Arnold Bennett's Fiction

Victorian & Edwardian Studies

Volume 8

Edited by
Francesco Marroni
"G. d'Annunzio" University of Chieti-Pescara

PETER LANG

Bern · Berlin · Bruxelles · New York · Oxford

Francesca D'Alfonso

Arnold Bennett's Fiction

From the Potteries to Literary Success

PETER LANG

Bern · Berlin · Bruxelles · New York · Oxford

Bibliographic Information published by the Deutsche Nationalbibliothek

The Deutsche Nationalbibliothek lists this publication in the Deutsche Nationalbibliografie; detailed bibliographic data is available in the internet at http://dnb.d-nb.de.

Library of Congress Cataloging-in-Publication Data
A CIP catalog record for this book has been applied for
at the Library of Congress.

Publication subsidized by the
Dipartimento Giuridico – Università degli Studi del Molise, Campobasso (Italy)

UNIVERSITÀ
DEGLI STUDI
DEL MOLISE

Cover illustration: Picture of Arnold Bennett, circa 1910

ISSN 1664-2104
ISBN 978-3-0343-4596-5 (Print)
E-ISBN 978-3-0343-4662-7 (E-PDF)
E-ISBN 978-3-0343-4663-4 (E-PUB)
DOI 10.3726/b20408

This publication has been peer reviewed.

© Peter Lang Group AG
International Academic Publishers, Bern 2023
bern@peterlang.com
All rights reserved.

www.peterlang.com

CONTENTS

PREFACE

In comparison with most English authors of his time, Arnold Bennett has found favour with very few literary critics. The reasons for this are not difficult to explain: Bennett had no qualms about exploiting his extraordinary narrative skills for purely economic purposes, regardless of the negative impact the huge output of his novels and short stories would have on the quality of his writing and (what was even more important), his image. Consequently, his literary activity was inevitably involved with the popular novel genre of the early nineteenth century which would, in turn, be taken up by sensation fiction in the sixties (see Wilkie Collins, M. E. Braddon, Ellen Wood, etc).

Bennett's figure has enjoyed a recent revival through the publication of Patrick Donovan's biography, after years of silence on the part of English and non-English critics alike, who, as Bernard Bergonzi has pointed out, had identified two almost divergent paths in the development of his art: "Bennett was a man of prodigious energy, who wrote fiction on two levels: in addition to those carefully planned novels which he regarded as serious works of art, he produced a great many books of a frankly pot-boiling kind in order to make money"[1]. In fact, Donovan describes Bennett as a "lost icon", i.e., an icon of the coeval cultural scene. However, it is often the case with artists who are all too visible during their lifetime, that they become – with very few exceptions – surrounded by a veil of silence after their death. As a result, Bennett has received very little critical attention. One remarkable exception worthy of mention is Margaret Drabble's biography which shows no hesitation in emphasising the greatness of his imaginative powers. Yet, as mentioned above, the critical neglect Bennett has suffered can be justified by the fact that he totally succumbed to the muse of commercialism. His all too free-flowing pen and all too fervid imagination,

---

1   Bernard Bergonzi, "The Advent of Modernism", in, *The Twentieth Century,* ed. Bernard Bergonzi, *Sphere History in the English Language*, 12 Vols., London, Sphere Books, 1970, Vol. VII, p. 26.

produced some eighty works, including novels, anthologies of short stories, essays and plays (some in collaboration with other writers), while in reality, only two novels and a few short stories have survived as classics of the Western canon.

For this reason, my study focuses on those works that are now considered authentic "classics" of European literature. Among these I have also included the novel *Accident*, which, to my mind, has been unfairly underrated by critics and reviewers. It is my view that in *Accident* Bennett achieves the levels of his best work, demonstrating an extraordinary ability to portray a world in which change was linked to the new means of transport. Furthermore, my monograph is not organised in terms of a chronological sequence with a discussion of all the writer's works, but follows a thematic development in which the Potteries and the young Bennett's desire to move away from a place that had nothing to offer him, apart from the monotony of its commerce and the work ethic of its inhabitants. In this context, it is particularly important to emphasise the figure of the artist who, as I try to make clear in each chapter, becomes the only means of revolt against the imaginative sterility of the Five Towns. In this sense, there is an overlap and convergence between the writer and certain biographical features of his protagonists, such as Sophia Baines who, with her escape to Paris, embodies the same rebelliousness that must have animated Arnold Bennett when – as described in Drabble's and Donovan's biographies – he felt the oppressive presence of a culturally confined and religiously narrow-minded microcosm that had nothing more to offer than a dreary industrial landscape and the worthless respectability of a community exclusively devoted to its industrial and commercial activities.

Before concluding this brief preface, I would like to express my utmost gratitude to Francesco Marroni, Director of the Victorian and Edwardian Studies series, a tireless scholar who has been my main wellspring of inspiration and learning for a quarter of a century now. He generously read and re-read my manuscript while never failing to provide me with methodological suggestions, critical insights and, above all, a genuine affection that I hope I have been able to reciprocate.

My deepest esteem also goes to Ruggiero Dipace, Director of the Department of Law of the University of Molise, for having encouraged and financed the publication of this volume, and always showing the signs of a wonderful friendship.

I am indebted to Giuseppe Peter Vanoli more than I could ever say, more than I could ever write, for believing in me and for keeping my spirits and motivation high with his enthusing closeness and support.

A very special thanks to Renzo D'Agnillo, who patiently and scrupulously read every chapter of this monograph, providing me with valuable advice on a stylistic level as well as discussing with me the most recent critical works on Bennett.

I am particularly grateful to Raffaella Antinucci, Luca Baratta, Francesca Caraceni, Michela Marroni, Enrichetta Soccio and Tania Zulli (please forgive the alphabetical order) with whom I have had numerous discussions on both a literary and personal level.

I would also like to mention the enthusiasm with which the members of the Arnold Bennett Society continue to dedicate their lively encounters, seminars and talks in order to promote the ideas and works of the author of the Potteries. Even though I have never been personally acquainted with them, their initiatives have greatly contributed in furthering my knowledge of the places in which Bennett lived.

Finally, I would like to thank my colleagues at the University of Molise who, although not involved in my field of research, have always been keen to hear about my interests across the channel.

This book is dedicated to my extraordinary students in the post-Graduate course in Literature and the History of Art in Molise.

Campobasso, 13.09.2022

CHAPTER 1   Fiction and realism
according to Arnold Bennett

1. One of the main features of Arnold Bennett's literary activity is the apparent discontinuity of his imaginative vision. His works seem to alternate too often between profound novels with a broad canvass and light-hearted tales fashioned for the demands of the literary market. He may well be the author of masterpieces which have left their mark on the nineteenth and twentieth century English novel, but the success he obstinately pursued could not be separated, for him, from his intention to reach out to as many readers as possible. For Bennett, however, this was not simply a case of financial profit but an indication of his ability to follow the pulse of English society while avoiding the detachment and loftiness which characterised most authors of the late Victorian and Edwardian periods. Thus, Bennett's quest for popularity and success was dictated not only by commercial ends but also by his deeply ingrained belief that the literary marketplace should be respected and acknowledged as a fundamental channel upon which the book industry depended for its existence.

In his 1903 essay on the novel, "The 'Average Reader' and the Recipe for Popularity", Bennett clearly outlines his ideas on the question of the circulation of novels:

> To admire the less admirable in art is not a crime, nor the fruit of a mischievous intention to overthrow the august verdict of the centuries: nor is it a mere vagary. If 50,000 people buy a novel whose shortcomings render it tenth-rate, we may be sure that they have not conspired to do so, and also that their apparently strange unanimity is not due to chance. There must be another explanation of the phenomenon, and when this explanation is discovered some real progress will have been made towards that democratisation of art which it is surely the duty of the minority to undertake, and to undertake in a religious spirit. The missionary does not make converts by a process of jeers; he minimises the difference between himself and the heathen, assumes a brotherhood, and sympathetically

leads forward from one point of view to another; and in order thus to lead forward
he finds out what the first point of view is[2].

The term to be underlined here is *democratisation*. For this is precisely what lies behind Bennett's polemic towards those authors of the
beginning of the twentieth century who represented the emergence of a
conception of art grounded on experimentation rather than the expectations of the reading public. Authors such as Henry James and Joseph
Conrad were paving the way for modernism as a reaction to Victorianism with their adoption of narrative techniques which dispensed with
the omniscient narrator, chronological linearity and straightforward-
ness of interpretation[3].

An important aspect of the present study concerns Bennett's analysis of the phenomenon of the 'average reader' precisely because the
writer attempts to clarify his views on the novel and its future prospects in terms of readership. The first important point to emerge is his
conviction that fiction will resist every kind of socioeconomic transformation and that, in time, it will become the most relevant literary form
provided that the reader's tastes are respected. Furthermore, it is also
interesting to note Bennett's awareness that the novel belongs to a category of writing that best interprets the values and disvalues of change
in an era in which everything seems to be continually transformed at
dazzling speed.

---

2   Arnold Bennett, *Fame and Fiction. An Enquiry into Certain Popularities*, Lon-
     don, Grant Richards, 1901, p. 5.
3   As Linda R. Williams writes: "The beginning of a century is not necessarily
     the century's *literary* beginning. It could, for instance, be argued that modernist
     writing actually began well into the century itself, and was engendered, was
     given its first breath, by war: English modernism emerged in its clearest form
     during the vast conflict of World War I, which gave the first kick to literary
     and artistic form self-consciously characterising themselves as 'modern' rather
     than 'Victorian'". Linda R. Williams, "Introduction: Writing from Modernism
     to Postmodernism", in *Bloomsbury Guide to English Literature: The Twentieth
     Century*, ed. Linda R. Williams, London, Bloomsbury, 1994, p. 7 (italics in
     the text). In the same volume, in his essay "Culture and Consciousness in the
     Twentieth-century novel", Andrew Roberts places James and Conrad as initia-
     tors of modernist sensibility in the subchapter "Culture and Reality: James and
     Conrad" (pp. 31–34).

Thus, in his defence of the traditional novel, Bennett accuses those who consider the genre from the point of view of a literary elite who prefer to ignore the preferences of the public in their sole intent to gratify their own view of the world and their feelings towards it. What is Bennett in fact saying when he compares the writer to a missionary whose aim is to convert the ignorant masses to the beauty of art? Although he mentions no names or refers to any specific literary or intellectual circle, he is obviously thinking of those contemporary literary figures who, in their pursuit of a form to convey the most rarefied nuances of life in an involuted and obscure style, devoid of the immediacy typical of traditional prose, were effectively distancing the reader from the narrative productions of this period. One of the authors Bennett has in mind is, without doubt, Henry James who, with his theory of the limited point of view, aimed to represent, as he himself writes in his "Preface" to *The Wings of the Dove*, the "supersubtleties, other arch-refinements, of tact and taste, of design and instinct"[4].

Bennett's attitude is that of a writer who absolutely refuses to accept the increasing distance of the public from the novel as a result of the inability of writers to interpret the feelings of the average reader. On the contrary, for Bennett, it is only by reducing such a gap as much as possible that the novel can be ensured a long life:

> Not only is art a factor in life; it is a factor in all lives. The division of the world into two classes, one of which has a monopoly of what is called "artistic feeling", is arbitrary and false. Everyone is an artist, more or less; that is to say, there is no person quite without that faculty of poetising, which by seeing beauty creates beauty, and which, when it is sufficiently powerful and articulate, constitutes the musical composer, the architect, the imaginative writer, the sculptor and

---

4   Henry James, *The Art of the Novel*, with an Introduction by R. P. Blackmur, New York, Charles Scribner's Sons, 1937. It is worthwhile giving the full quotation in its original context. "[...] my use of windows and balconies is doubtless at best an extravagance by itself, and as to what there may be to note, of this and other supersubtleties, other arch-refinements, of tact and taste, of design and instinct, in *The Wings of the Dove*, I become conscious of overstepping my space without having brought the full quantity to light" (p. 306). For an analysis of James' techniques as presented in his prefaces to his narrative works, see Francesco Marroni, "'A Great Grey Void': Henry James, le 'Prefaces' e i sentieri della critica", *Letterature d'America*, 19–20, 83–84 (1999–2000), pp. 31–58.

the painter. To the persistent ignoring of this obvious truth is due much misunderstanding and some bitterness. The fault lies originally with the minority, the more artistic, which has imposed an artificial distinction upon the majority, the less artistic[5].

Bennett's intention is evidently to break down the barrier separating the public at large from artistic works. If art is to be such an important element for human beings as to be part of their physical and spiritual relationship with the world, any subdivisions appear to Bennett the product of a cultural artifice and the manipulation of ideas impossible to accept. His indignation is all the fiercer for what he considers to be a false opposition between high and low literature, which implies an analogous contrast between a culturally and, often, economically privileged minority and a majority apparently incapable of appreciating refined works of art.

Acutely aware of the fact that he himself came from a non-literary family[6] in which no member displayed any particular artistic inclinations whatsoever[7], Bennett felt the need to bridge the existing gap

---

5   Bennett, *op. cit.*, p. 3.
6   Bennett's family, which had a draper's shop, had almost no connections with literature. After working as a labourer and then as *master potter* in the local industry, his father, Enoch Bennett, not without great sacrifices, became a solicitor at the age of 29. Arnold was born in Henley in the Staffordshire Potteries. He attended school until he was sixteen and then moved to London to work as a clerk at a firm of solicitors. Through hard work and discipline, he made his mark on the literary world in London for his unquestionable skills as a narrator. As John Wain writes, "he began tamely enough with a secondary school education and a grounding in law in his father's office. At the age of twenty-one he moved to London, to take a job as a shorthand clerk with a firm of solicitors. One step at a time! He had behind him some small successes in local journalism, and he had a general willingness to use his pen to make extra money, if this proved feasible". John Wain, "Introduction", in Arnold Bennett, *The Old Wives's Tale*, London, Penguin, 2007, p. 9.
7   Cf. Margaret Drabble, *Arnold Bennett: A Biography*, London, Weidenfeld and Nicolson, 1974, pp. 23–46. On the writer's origins, Drabble observes: "There is not very much to be gained from tracing the Bennett family ancestry in detail. It was not distinguished – as in so many English families, the majority were hard-working unnoticeable people, in this case mostly potters, rent-collectors, shopkeepers. Some combined potting and shopkeeping" (p. 23).

between the popular novel and narrative works which were more markedly experimental and primarily designed to challenge the Victorian novel.

As Barbara and Giorgio Melchiori have observed, Henry James (1843–1916) was conscious of "that sense of the fundamental ambiguity of the feelings and nature of man" and as a consequence envisaged "the triumph of the point of view technique, of the subtle manner of representing with caution and deftness at the same time people and events from the point of view of one or more observers who highlight the diverse facets of the same subject, deforming it further according to its own nature"[8]. Born twenty-four years before Bennett, James confronted the problem of representing the veiled aspects of human nature. Thus, elusiveness and ambiguity become the hallmarks of his renewal of the novel in which the point of view adopted is inevitably that of a character who can only offer a partial view of reality and, therefore, of the truth. Needless to say, Modernist approaches from the experimental prose of Virginia Woolf to the fragmented images of the poetry of T.S. Eliot would follow along the same lines.

In opposition to this line of experimentation, Bennett, like most Victorian authors, particularly George Eliot and Charles Dickens – favours the technique of the omniscient narrator. His respect for the reader and his conviction that the novel cannot be separated from the idea of reading for pleasure, are only confirmation for him that the choice of techniques based on indirection broaden the gap between high-brow and popular literature which he wanted to eliminate altogether.

From another angle, during the last years of the nineteenth century, a writer like Thomas Hardy had realised that the novel was no longer able to represent what he called "the modern vice of unrest"[9]. In fact, after the publication of *Jude the Obscure* in 1895, Hardy decided to abandon novel writing since he considered its sociocultural function to be surpassed, given the fact that the literary conventions and expressive tools adopted by Victorian writers were completely inadequate in

---

8   Barbara and Giorgio Melchiori, *Il gusto di Henry James*, Torino, Einaudi, 1974, p. 159.

9   Thomas Hardy, *Jude the Obscure*, ed. Patricia Ingham, Oxford, Oxford University Press, 2008, p. 79.

dealing with the radical changes in English society[10]. To be more precise, he no longer believed the novel to be the best form through which to render the complexities of the modern human condition. Consequently, for the remaining years of his life, he devoted himself exclusively to writing poetry.

At opposite poles of the lively debate around the novel between the end of the nineteenth and beginning of the twentieth century are those who, on the one hand, declare the death of the traditional novel and, on the other, writers who believe there can be a future for this literary genre if there is a different way of conceiving the relationship between author and reader and the literary tastes of the age. Clearly, Bennett, who is completely convinced that the novel is anything but finished, belongs to the latter category. However, in his case, he assigns the novel a two-fold social function: firstly, as a form of entertainment, as reading for pleasure; secondly, as a moral teaching with a didactic design to instruct the reading public about the ways of the world.

With Henry James the case is rather different. Although he firmly believes in the art of the novel, he often underlines the fact that it should adhere more to reality, not in a naturalistic sense, but more precisely in terms of a closer representation of the subtle psychological connections, rarefied mental predicaments and interior landscapes that characterise human beings. James has no doubts regarding the opposition between showing and telling: the narrator must show what happens without interpreting it and without explaining to the reader what happens behind appearances. Percy Lubbock, one of the best interpreters of James' method, specifies this feature in his discussion of *The Ambassadors* (1903) and the dilemmas of its protagonist Lambert Strether:

> The novelist, more free than the playwright, could of course *tell* us, if he chose, what lurks behind this agitated spirit; he could step forward and explain the restless appearance of the man's thought. But if he prefers the dramatic way, admittedly the more effective, there is nothing to prevent him from taking it. The man's thought, in its turn, can be made to reveal its own inwardness[11].

---

10   Cf. Francesco Marroni, "Thomas Hardy e la 'fine' del romanzo vittoriano", *RSV: Rivista di Studi Vittoriani*, 8, 16 (Luglio 2003), pp. 11–23.

11   Percy Lubbock, *The Craft of Fiction*, New York, Viking, 1972 [1st ed. 1957], pp. 157–158 (italics in the text).

In drawing his technique from drama, therefore, the writer must priori-
tise showing over telling, in other words, abandon the story told by the
omniscient narrator that is typical of the Victorian novel. For James,
form was much too important to be treated superficially. The novel form
must always be questioned and never considered as a passive vehicle to
be manipulated willy-nilly but as a living entity through which to dramatize the tortuous paths of the human psyche according to the various
manifestations of life. In his theory of the novel, James has some very
important things to say in terms of its revaluation and reaffirmation: "A
novel is a living thing, all one and continuous, like any other organism,
and in proportion as it lives will it be found, that in each of the parts
there is something of each of the other parts"[12]. James's organic view
of the novel is undoubtedly derived from the great French tradition,
notably Flaubert and Maupassant, whom he cites as exemplary models.
In this respect, he assumes a polemic stance towards the English and
American productions of this period which were still conditioned by
the narrative strategies typical of Victorian writers. It goes without
saying that the organic theory entails that every part of a novel must be
connected and that there must be no section or segment that does not
have a relevance to the other parts of the story. As Peter Keating writes,
James is opposed to "the Victorian 'pudding' view of fiction, with its
implied mixture of good things often irrelevant to the whole experience
but nice for the taster"[13]. For the American writer, the great Victorian
novels were imposing narrative machines in which many threads, in
the end, were left broken and much material was lost precisely because
of a lack of unity and organic design in which to include and harmonise
the parts of the whole.

   From this point of view, James's criticism against Bennett, however indirect, is obvious: Bennett appears to be a writer who is totally
convinced that the best way to narrate a story is that which for decades

---

12   Henry James, "The Art of Fiction" in Walter Besant, *The Art of Fiction*,
     New York, Cupples, Upham and Company, 1885, p. 68. The second part of this
     American edition dedicated to Besant's essay contains Henry James's reply. The
     title is the same as Besant's: "The Art of Fiction", pp. 51–85.
13   J.P. Keating, *The Haunted Study. A Social History of the English Novel 1875–
     1914*, London, Fontana Press, 1991, p. 112.

has distinguished the Victorian novel. In a similar way to Bennett, the popular writer Walter Besant had provoked the reaction of Henry James by claiming the right of the novel to face moral questions in line with the great tradition of George Eliot and Charles Dickens. Drawing on English positivism, Besant was convinced that a story unable to arouse the sympathy and understanding of its readers had no reason to exist because its framework should always be provided with a solid and transparent moral design: "The modern novel converts abstract ideas into living models; it gives ideas, it strengthens faith, it preaches a higher morality than is seen in the actual world; it commands the emotions of pity, admiration, and terror; it creates and keeps alive the sense of sympathy; it is the universal teacher"[14]. Even though he is of the same generation as Henry James, Besant effectively finds himself in the opposing camp because his idea of the art of fiction is both militant and moralistic. By declaring the novel to be a universal teacher he foregrounds its didactic valence which, for Henry James, can only be a consequence ultimately derived from the author himself. As Mark Spilka notes, if there is a point of convergence between James and Besant it concerns the comparison of the art of fiction to painting:

> James's fascination with the painting analogy is a case in point. Besant had repeatedly compared fiction with painting and had borrowed its terminology to advance his arguments. James would do likewise. But where Besant pressed for the exact correspondence between 'the laws of harmony, perspective, and proportion', which governed both arts, James pressed for a common purpose: the

---

14   Walter Besant, *op. cit.*, p. 10. In his reply, James rejoices over the fact that a promising debate on the novel has begun, particularly because in the decades dominated by figures such as Dickens and Thackeray such a debate would have seemed unthinkable: "During the period I have alluded to there was a comfortable, good-humoured feeling abroad that a novel is a novel, as a pudding is a pudding, and that this was the end of it. But within a year or two, for some reason or other, there have been signs of returning animation – the era of discussion would appear to have been to a certain extent opened. *Art lives upon discussion, upon experiment, upon curiosity, upon variety of attempt, upon the exchange of views and the comparison of standpoints*" (James, "The Art of Fiction", cit., p. 52, my italics). It seems obvious that James is distancing himself from Besant here since the latter did not believe either in experimentation or the crucial function of a theoretical discussion on the narratological aspects of the novel.

'attempt to represent life'. Originally, James had called it an attempt to 'compete with life'[15].

It seems evident, therefore, that in Besant's interpretation the connection between the novel and painting is confirmed by the fact that the two art forms are based on the same aesthetic laws[16]. James's more general idea is that there is a tension common to fiction and painting to "represent life". From James's point of view, a writer always represents his relationship with the world in all its moral implications but never prioritises its ethical design: "We are discussing the Art of Fiction; questions of art are questions (in the widest sense) of execution; questions of morality are quite another affair"[17]. In exactly the same way as Besant, Bennett was convinced that the taste of the reading public should navigate the writer just like a compass. As Anderson has noted, James, in anticipating the tensions of modernism, took the opposite view:

> James rejected popular taste as an accurate guide as to what 'good' fiction should be because, unlike Besant, the reading public did not for him represent a

---

15 Mark Spilka, *op. cit.*, p. 115.

16 Obviously, the problem of representation in the novel is part of a broader discussion which, in many ways, can be traced back to Ruskin's *word-painting*. Besides, it is also true that Horace had formulated the expression *Ut pictura poësis*, to point out that a poem must be like a painting. Whatever the case, the search for a narrative method to give priority to the visible involved various writers, among whom Robert Louis Stevenson and Joseph Conrad. It is precisely this form of realism based on the visible that led to modernist aesthetics in which the language of the visible (i.e., the language that renders things visible) prevailed over the authorial intervention and omniscience typical of the Victorian novel. It is no accident that in 1922, Joyce, in *Ulysses* would speak of "the ineluctable modality of the visibile". James Joyce, *Ulysses*, ed. Hans Walter Gabler with Wolfhard Steppe and Claus Melchior, Harmondsworth, Penguin, 1986, p. 31.

17 James, "The Art of Fiction", cit., p. 81. James allows Besant the possibility of a moral dimension to a story in the following terms: "There is one point at which the moral sense and the artistic sense lie very near together; that is in the light of the very obvious truth that the deepest quality of a work of art will always be the quality of the mind of the producer" (p. 83).

community who shared similar values but the 'mass' who were to be feared as
the repository of the commonplace, the second-rate, the trivial[18].

For Bennett, whose imagination had been stimulated by the novels
of Ouida, (at that time the most popular writer in the English literary
scene) there was something absurd about James's conception of the
novel. From his point of view, contempt of the marketplace and the
reading choices of the public was equivalent to commercial suicide. If
it was true that James belonged to one of the richest and most powerful
families in New York, it was not the same case for Bennett. As a man
from the north of England who grew up in the potteries, he could not
allow himself the luxury of ignoring the public. Neither did he intend to
renounce the idea that a writer's job, if he was talented, could be highly
profitable.

2. The writer who launched the most direct attack against Bennett's approach to the art of fiction was probably Virginia Woolf. Her
own radical renewal of narrative form and technique, through which
she created an atmosphere of ambiguity and moral relativism, is very
similar to that of James who, some decades before Woolf, had based his
fiction on the limited point of view. In their discussion of Woolf's artistic approach Malcolm Bradbury and James McFarlane observe: "[n]ow
human consciousness and especially *artistic* consciousness could
become more intuitive, more poetic; art could now fulfil itself. It was
free to catch at the manifold – the atoms as they fall [...]"[19]. For Woolf
it was not only a question of representing the ambivalence of real life in
all its nuances, but also of giving verbal representation to the thoughts
of the characters as they arise and are discarded in their consciousness
and highlighting their intuitions and moments of epiphany as much as
their moments of darkness. In other words, writing becomes a tool with
which to conduct an intense investigation of the human soul and its
relationship to others and the world in general: "The modern novel thus
becomes the novel of fine consciousness; it escapes the conventions of

---

18   Linda R. Anderson, *Bennett, Wells and Conrad: Narrative in Transition*,
     New York, St Martin's Press, 1988, p. 10.
19   Malcolm Bradbury and James McFarlane, "The Name and Nature of Mod-
     ernism", in *Modernism: A Guide to European Literature 1890–1930*, ed. Malcolm
     Bradbury and James McFarlane, London and New York, Penguin, 1991, p. 25.

fact-giving and story-telling; it desubstantiates the material world and puts it in its just place; it transcends the vulgar limitations and simplicities of realism, so as to serve a higher realism"[20]. Woolf does not so much demand that the techniques of realism should be abandoned than suggest a form of realism rendered through the consciousness which is more intent on rendering internal rather than external action. Thus, although external reality is not entirely disregarded, it is undoubtedly subordinated to the point of view of her characters.

Along the lines of these technical, theoretical and ideological assumptions, Woolf read a paper at The Heretics Club in Cambridge on 18 May 1924 (which she had already published in a journal a year earlier) titled "Mr. Bennett and Mrs. Brown"[21]. The central part of her paper contains a strong disapproval of Bennett's narrative methods which she sees as quintessential of Edwardian authors such as, besides Bennett, H.G. Wells (1866–1946) and John Galsworthy (1867–1933)[22]. She particularly reproaches Edwardian writers for the fact that in their excessive attention to the tastes of the general public and lack of interest in experimentation they betray a disinclination to detach themselves from the Victorian tradition

At the very beginning of her conference, Woolf launches her first attack quoting Bennett's own words regarding the diegetic centrality of the character:

> My belief that men and women write novels because they are lured on to create some character which has thus imposed itself upon them has the sanction of Mr. Arnold Bennett. In an article from which I will quote he says, "The foundation of good fiction is character-creating and nothing else... Style counts; plot counts; originality of outlook counts. But none of these counts anything like so much as the convincingness of the characters. If the characters are real the novel will have a chance; if they are not, oblivion will be its portion..." And he goes on to

---

20 John Fletcher and Malcolm Bradbury, "The Introverted Novel", in *Modernism: A Guide to European Literature 1890–1930*, cit., p. 408.

21 Virginia Woolf, "Mr. Bennett and Mrs. Brown" in *Collected Essays*, ed. Leonard Woolf, London, Chatto and Windus, 1966, pp. 319–337. Henceforth all quotations refer to this edition and are indicated in the text as *BB* followed by page numbers.

22 The dates of the authors are provided to indicate the fact that they belonged to the very same generation.

draw the conclusion that we have no young novelists of first-rate importance at the present moment, because they are unable to create characters that are real, true, and convincing (*BB*, p. 319).

The fact that Bennett declares that the modern generations of writers are incapable of creating real and convincing characters did not fail to provoke a response from Virginia Woolf who attempts in every way possible to reverse the accusation in order to show that it is precisely Bennett and other Edwardian writers who are incapable of creating credible portraits based on a realistic observation of human beings. For Woolf, only the new narrators – the exponents of modernism – are able to represent authentic characters who move and speak like real human beings. Woolf demands that factual superfluities[23] be eliminated in order to give precedence to psychological representation in order to penetrate the obscure pathways of the human consciousness. To support her thesis, the writer adopts an argumentative strategy that aims to directly involve the reader in answering the central questions of her essay: what does character mean? In narrative terms, how can a character be described in such a way as to appear real before our eyes? To what extent can a character be considered credible? What should an author's attitude be in presenting a particular character in a novel? Such are the questions Woolf attempts to answer in "Mr. Bennett and Mrs. Brown".

In her discussion of the literary creation of character, Woolf does not adopt the abstract approach of critical theory but imagines herself in a railway carriage with a woman whom, for convenience sake, she chooses to call by the deliberately banal and common name of Mrs Brown:

> She was one of those clean, threadbare old ladies whose extreme tidiness – everything buttoned, fastened, tied together, mended and brushed up – suggests more extreme poverty than rags and dirt. There was something pinched about her – a look of suffering, of apprehension, and, in addition, she was extremely small. Her feet, in their clean little boots, scarcely touched the floor (*BB*, p. 322).

---

23 Flora de Giovanni, "Virginia Woolf e le arti" in Virginia Woolf, *Immagini/Pictures*, translation and introduction by Flora de Giovanni, Napoli, Liguori Editore, 2002, p. 11.

Woolf proceeds to conduct her analysis in terms of her creative imagination describing the woman's physical aspect in detail including her facial expression and the impressions she conveys with her small, defenceless and almost contracted body. Although the writer imagines herself to be in the same carriage, no dialogue actually takes place between them. At this point, however, the silence triggers in Woolf a series of story lines:

> *I felt that* she had nobody to support her; that she had to make up her mind for herself; that, having been deserted, or left a widow, years ago, she had led an anxious, harried life, bringing up an only son, perhaps, who, as likely as not, was by this time beginning to go to the bad. All this shot through my mind as I sat down, being uncomfortable, like most people, at travelling with fellow passengers unless I have somehow or other accounted for them. Then I looked at the man. He was no relation of Mrs. Brown's *I felt sure*; he was of a bigger, burlier, less refined type. He was a man of business *I imagined*, very likely a respectable corn-chandler from the North, dressed in good blue serge with a pocket-knife and a silk handkerchief, and a stout leather bag. Obviously, however, he had an unpleasant business to settle with Mrs. Brown; a secret, perhaps sinister business, which they did not intend to discuss in my presence (*BB*, p. 322, my italics).

With such phrases as *I felt, I felt sure, I imagined*, Woolf is indicating the potential stories that the figure of Mrs Brown suggests. Therefore, she is any woman who becomes, in the context of a railway journey, the protagonist of an event that Woolf is engaged in deciphering. Nevertheless, in the absence of the omniscient voice of the Victorian novel, the writer is forced to construct her character on the basis of the woman's visible signs. In this respect, what is visible becomes the point of departure. At the same time the scene becomes more dynamic with the introduction of Mr Smith, the commercial traveller from the north, who triggers further suggestions in Woolf's mind.

At this point Woolf feels the urge to understand the nature of the relationship between Mrs Brown and Mr Smith which seems all the more stimulating for the fact that their respective personalities suggest a somewhat mysterious connection: "a secret, perhaps sinister business". The word *perhaps* points to the indiscernibility of a story which a novelist like Dickens or Trollope, whose adoption of the omniscient narrator would have openly revealed the woman's distressed mind, would have had no difficulty in relating. The modernist novelist, on the other hand, is only left to imagine or guess. In fact, the following dialogue – an example of what James defines as *showing* – offers the writer further elements in order to construct her narrative through the tiny clues which emerge and to develop the behavioural traits of the character of Mrs Brown. In this way, Woolf is ready to write a novel about a woman she meets in a railway carriage and explore her inner world in terms of what she has seen and heard. As a result, Woolf "laments the inability of the Edwardian novelists to see the 'reality', the inner life, of the legendary Mrs. Brown"[24] and imagining what Bennett's approach would be, observes:

> Mr. Bennett, alone of the Edwardians, would keep his eyes on the carriage. He, indeed, would observe every detail with immense care. He would notice the advertisements, the pictures of Swanage and Portsmouth; the way in which the cushion bulged between the buttons; how Mrs. Brown wore a brooch which had cost three-and-ten-three at Whitworth's bazar; and had mended both gloves – indeed the thumb of the left-hand glove had been replaced. And he would observe, at length, how this was the nonstop train from Windsor which calls at Richmond for the convenience of middle-class residents, who can afford to go to the theatre but have not reached the social rank which can afford motor-cars, though it is true, there are occasions (he would tell us which) (*BB*, p. 328).

As Robert Squillace has noted: "An obsession with 'surface value' was the charge most frequently levelled at Bennett by critics who believed he never comprehended any but traditionally realist methods of writing fiction"[25]. After showing the particular care with which Bennett observes the external world, even from the window of a railway carriage, Woolf concludes her hostile analysis by declaring that the author of *Anna of the Five* towns would be so engrossed in describing every aspect of the external scene as to completely forget the existence of a Mrs Brown. In other words, the protagonist of the scene who should be at the centre of his attention would be simply ignored:

---

24   Patricia Ondek Laurence, *The Reading of Silence: Virginia Woolf in the English Tradition*, Stanford, CA, Stanford University Press, 1991, p. 17.
25   Robert Squillace, *Modernism, Modernity, and Arnold Bennett*, Lewisburg, Bucknell University Press; London, Associated University Press, 1997, p. 25.

I have formed my own opinion of what Mr. Bennett is about – he is trying to make us imagine for him; he is trying to hypnotize us into the belief that, because he has made a house, there must be a person living there. With all his powers of observation, which are marvellous, with all his sympathy and humanity, which are great, *Mr. Bennett has never once looked at Mrs. Brown in her corner* (*BB*, p. 330, my italics).

In her demolition of Bennett's narrative method and style, Woolf adopts an argumentative strategy in which she avoids revealing her own modernist ideas. Through a subtle form of understatement, she praises his powers of observation while evidencing the negative fact that such powers are limited to topological features rather than being used to offer an adequate representation of character. In Woolf's eyes, a house, according to Bennett's conception, must contain a person and must be the place where voices, feelings and stories are interwoven once it has been described. Consequently, the excessive attention to the description of the external and internal dimensions of a house would be enough to satisfy Bennett's desire for realism. In Woolf's view, Bennett's detailed descriptions of objects, far from developing a character's thoughts or inner world are only a waste of words which drastically diminish the impact of the story.

Despite Woolf's acute arguments, Bennett's case, in reality, is quite different. It may be granted that he would describe the house scrupulously in every detail, but he would also provide a detailed physical and psychological description of the character. Woolf is wrong to claim that Mrs Brown would be left abandoned in the corner of the railway carriage by a writer completely indifferent to her physiognomy, thoughts, emotions and gestures. For his very technique consists in the meticulous focalisation of characters in their environment. In other words, Bennett's main objective is to offer the reader a text (i.e., character) and a context (i.e., aspects of the external world).

On the other hand, there is a consolidated critical tradition that recognises a precise link between characters and the spaces they occupy. As Wellek and Warren observe: "A man's house is an extension of himself"[26]. Therefore, it cannot be said that the protagonist of a scene

---

26 René Wellek and Austin Warren, *Theory of Literature*, New York, Harcourt, Brace and Company, 1949, p. 229.

has nothing to do with the house in which they live and the objects that surround them. Woolf's concept of character, in this respect, appears to be rather radical in her prejudice against Bennett. In her critical interpretation the idea of a writer whose gaze lingers on every detail and completely neglects the figure of an apparently insignificant woman in a railway carriage must remain in the foreground.

As Squillace has rightly observed, this insistence on the separation between the individual and the environment implies that Bennett is incapable of presenting a character in all its humanity: "Woolf provides the most carefully developed version of the argument, claiming that Bennett failed to invest his meticulously observed physical detail with enough inconvenient humanity to give them any but a documentary significance"[27]. From Bennett's point of view, Woolf's criticism is entirely inappropriate because he is convinced that the discourse on the form of the novel – with its consequent themes concerning artistic exploration in general – is certainly not a factor to be neglected. It must be recalled that even in 1910 Bennett insisted on the importance of French authors who had always placed at the centre of their exploration a reflection on the formal aspects of fiction. More precisely, in a review of a book by Sturge Moore[28] which appeared in the journal *New Age*, Bennett makes the following reflections on the state of the novel:

> His value is that he would make the English artist a conscious artist. He does, without once stating it, bring out in the most startling way the contrast between, for example, the English artist and the Continental artist. Read the correspondence of Dickens and Thackeray, and then read the correspondence of Flaubert, and you will see. The latter was continually preoccupied with his craft, the two former scarcely ever – and never in an intelligent fashion. I have been preaching on this theme for years, but I am not aware that anybody has been listening. I was going to say that I was sick of preaching about it, but I am not. I shall continue [...][29].

---

27   Squillace, *op. cit.*, p. 25.
28   Sturge Moore (1870–1944) was a poet much appreciated in the first decades of the twentieth century. In fact, he was a candidate for the post of "Poet Laureate". It may be interesting to add here that the brother of the philosopher George Edward Moore was also a part of the Bloomsbury Group, founded by Woolf among other intellectual figures.
29   Arnold Bennett, "Books and Persons", *New Age*, VI (24 March 1910), p. 494.

As clearly emerges from the quotation above, Bennett's position seems to be in accord with such modernist figures as James, Conrad and Ford Maddox Ford. His insistence on the importance of artistic awareness, together with the quotation from Flaubert, find him on the same wavelength as the great reformers who felt the need to abandon the Victorian notion of the novel which reflected ways of being and thinking that were considered completely outdated. In light of Bennett's critical reflections, Samuel Hynes believes his place should not be with those writers who continued to relate to the styles of the nineteenth century: "[...] his place among Edwardian novelists is with the Conscious Artist, and not with Galsworthy and Wells. If this is true, then ironically he belongs among the literary ancestors of Virginia Woolf"[30].

Only a reader unaware of Bennett's theoretical positions could define him as a writer attached artistically and ideologically to the Victorian period. From his earliest works, he was mainly influenced by naturalism which, however, he did not absorb without criticism. Indeed, the problem he felt most acutely was precisely how to overcome the Victorian novel – which he wanted to accomplish without disregarding the realist tradition and its representation of the "totality of objects", as Georg Lukács defines it[31]. In this respect, Bennett believes that the

---

30   Samuel Hynes, "The Whole Contention between Mr. Bennett and Mrs. Woolf", *Novel*, 1, 1 (Autumn 1967), p. 36. In his article, Hynes evidences how Bennett and Woolf were very different authors from both a biographical point of view and in terms of their personalities.: "Clearly Bennett and Mrs. Woolf were antithetical in all the important particulars of their personalities. It is equally obvious, I think, that they were *not* antithetical in their view of their common art. Their quarrel, when it came, rose out of their personal differences, and not out of their aesthetic convictions; but it soon lost definition, and became an untidy and bitter wrangle that marred both their lives for more than a decade" (p. 36, italics in the text).

31   See Georg Lukács, *The Historical Novel*, transl. by Hannah and Staley Mitchell, London, Merlin Press, 1989. In particular, Georg Lukács observes: "Hence things precisely because they depend on, and are permenently related to, the activity of men not only become important and significant, but thereby acquire their artistic independence as objects of representation. The demand for a 'totality of objects' in epic is essentially a demand for an artistic image of human society which peoduces and reproduces itself in the same way as the daily process of life", p. 93.

novel has a right to deal with the daily life of a protagonist showing both the psychology and the movements of the psyche in time together with the dramatization of the relevant semiotic signs which contribute to the definition of that daily life of which the writer must be the interpreter, if his main aim is to observe reality as close as possible. This is the narrative strategy of realism for Bennett which certainly would not exclude Mrs Brown from his observation – as Woolf tendentiously claims – but rather present her within the broadest context possible including a consideration of objects close up (the way the woman is dressed, her bags and her hairstyle) in the distance (the landscape seen from the window, the climate, the people in the station, the sounds coming from outside and everything which helps to define the environment).

In this dialectic between internal and external space, a character, from Bennett's point of view, takes on a complexity that is both psychological and material, invisible (internal world) and visible (external world). Besides, as Samuel Hynes notes, the beginning of the twentieth century signals a new way of interpreting character which was also due to the influence of Russian literature of which Henry James was a constant devotee:

> During the Edwardian years, two things had happened: first, sensitive men had become aware of the iniquities of the Victorian social system; and second, Mrs. Garnett's translations of Dostoevsky had appeared. Social awareness turned novelists into reformers; Dostoevsky destroyed their conventional notions of what a "character" was[32].

The transformation of the novel at the beginning of the century explains why works like James Joyce's *Ulysses* and Virginia Woolf's *Jacob's Room* were published in 1922[33]. This new phase of Modernism somehow includes Arnold Bennett, with all the reservations he

---

32   Hynes, *op. cit.*, p. 38.
33   James McFarlane, "The Mind of Modernism", in *Modernism: A Guide to European Literature 1890–1930*, cit., astutely evidences one of the aspects which render modernist attitudes so distant from Bennett's way of relating with the real world: "What is distinctive – and difficult – about the Modernist mode is that it seems to demand the reconciliation of two distinct ways of reconciling contradictions, ways which in themselves are also contrary. On the one hand, it recognizes the validity of a largely rational, Hegelian synthesis, a higher unity

held towards narrative productions which presented unsolved enigmas, impenetrable mysteries of the soul and repeated interpretative enigmas. Bennett also believes in the central role of the reader while, for Woolf, Joyce and other modernists the reader becomes an external presence and ultimately unimportant to the creative process.

3. The influence of naturalism on Bennett's works acted as a counterbalance to his friction with modernism. Besides representing a fundamental moment in his development as a realist novelist, it seemed to him to represent the right direction for his literary exploration. In this respect, he was following in the footsteps of George Gissing who was one of the first English novelists to look towards France for new ideas. Already in 1884 Gissing recognised the superiority of French literature: "English novels are miserable stuff for a very miserable reason, simply because English novelists fear to do their best lest they should damage their popularity and consequently their income [...] Let novelists be true to their artistic conscience"[34]. The author of *Demos* was posing a dilemma many novelists were facing and one that was also to torment Bennett: to become an author at the service of editors in the pursuit of popularity and wealth, or to make one's writing activity a mission and, consequently, live in poverty and ignore the demands of the literary marketplace and the preferences of less demanding readers. As has been seen, Bennett had no particular qualms in this respect. He did not consider the reading public as a motive for sleepless nights or as a financial threat. He had very clear ideas about what he wanted: it was simply a question of reconciling his literary exploration with the tastes of the public. Nevertheless, he drew a line beyond which there was no room for any form of compromise. This did not mean that he had renounced realism or repudiated his French influences, only that he wanted to give more prominence to the plot and not conceive his characters as unsolved or unsolvable enigmas.

---

which preserves the essence of the two conflicting elements whilst at the same time destroying them as separate entities" (pp. 87–88).

34　George Gissing, Lettera inviata al *Pall Mall Gazette* (15 December 1884). Cit. in Pierre Coustillas, *The Heroic Life of George Gissing*, 3 vols., London, Pickering & Chatto, 2011, *Part I: 1857–1888*, p. 251.

As emerges in most of his narrative productions, Bennett conceives his characters as ontologically and socially mobile entities, human beings who, as time passes, change in terms of their physical and psychological features. Indeed, Bennett almost always establishes, through the imaginative exploration of his omniscient narrator, a very powerful connection between character and time. As E. M. Forster has acutely observed: "Time is the real hero of *The Old Wives's Tale*. He is installed as the lord of creation [...] Sophia and Constance are the children of time from the instant we see them romping with their mother's dress; they are doomed to decay with a completeness that is very rare in literature"[35]. It appears evident that the writer in no sense considers the technique of the omniscient narrator as a burden to shake off, but an indispensable tool through which to focalise the sense of completeness Forster intends.

Bennett felt the urge to discover a way to mediate between the demands of the marketplace and those of literary honesty and coherence. He was often defined as a naturalist novelist but he refused the label for all the limitations it implied. Nevertheless, he was always ready to subscribe to one aspect of the naturalist method, that of the principle of observation and appropriation of reality even when it appears obscure and ambiguous – which was in line with what Zola wrote in his important essay *Le roman expérimental* in 1880[36]:

---

35   E. M. Forster, *Aspects of the Novel*, Harmondsworth, Penguin, 1972, p. 45.
36   As regards the presence of Émile Zola on the late-Victorian literary scene see J. P. Keating, *The Working Classes in Victorian Fiction* (cit.). For a precise idea of Zola's influence and the impact of *Le roman expérimental*, it may be useful to read the chapter "French naturalism and English working-class fiction" (pp. 125–138). According to Keating, the writer who follows the example of French naturalism most rigorously is George Moore, Bennett's friend and author of *Esther Waters* (1894), which many critics consider to be one of the most important novels of the late nineteenth century: "The symbolic structure of *Esther Waters* owes everything to Zola" (p. 134). It is no accident that in a letter dated 24 December 1920 Bennett confesses to Moore that he gave him the idea of placing the Potteries at the centre of his novels: "[...] I wish to tell you that it was the first chapters of *A Mummer's Wife* which opened my eyes to the romantic nature of the district that I had blindly inhabited for over twenty years. You are indeed the father of all my Five Towns books". *Letters of Arnold Bennett*, ed. James Hepburn, 4 vols., London, Oxford University Press, 1968, III, p. 139.

[...] les romanciers naturalistes observent et expérimentent, et que toute leur besogne naît du doute où ils se placent en face des vérités mal connues, des phénomènes inexpliqués, jusqu'à ce qu'une idée expérimentale éveille brusquement un jour leur génie et les pousse à instituer une expérience, pour analyser les faits et s'en rendre les maîtres[37].

Zola continues:

Le romancier expérimentateur est donc celui qui accepte les faits prouvés, qui montre dans l'homme et dans la société le mécanisme des phénomènes dont la science est maîtresse, et qui ne fait intervenir son sentiment personnel que dans les phénomènes dont le déterminisme n'est point encore fixé, en tâchant de contrôler le plus qu'il le pourra ce sentiment personnel, cette idée *a priori*, par l'observation et par l'expérience[38].

The two quotations, which are justly famous, offer a most effective explanation of Zola's equation between literature and science, the "romancier expérimentateur" and the scientist. As the French author observes, it is a question of method. While Bennett would never have supported the equation proposed in *Le roman expérimental*, he was willing to accept the idea that a narrator must work as precisely as possible and avoid creating ambiguities and doubts which are so essential in the writings of authors such as James and Woolf who, although they represent different generations, share the same intent to dispel with the technique of omniscience. It goes without saying that the omniscient narrative voice adopted by Bennett, as in Zola, is conferred with the power of knowing everything, of controlling the storyline and entering the minds of every character. What really differentiates Bennett's works from those authors more closely connected with naturalism is their themes. In fact, as Furst and Skrine have written, "Whatever their motives, the Naturalists did choose poverty, deprivation and squalor for their subject matter far more than any of their predecessors"[39]. It is not that Bennett ignores poverty as such, but he undoubtedly does not place the characteristic themes of naturalism at the centre of his literary imagination

---

37   Émile Zola, *Le roman expérimental*, Paris, Garnier-Flammarion, 1971, p. 67.
38   *Ibid.*, p. 96.
39   Lilian R. Furst and Peter N. Skrine, *Naturalism*, London, Methuen, 1971, p. 50.

Therefore, Bennett's literary technique must be seen within the context of early twentieth-century realism. In this sense, his conception of the novel is undoubtedly remote from the moralism characteristic of Victorian narratives since, for him, the moral must reside in the story itself. It is no accident that Fraser acutely observes, "Arnold Bennett has nothing of the high moral tone, the vague but real distress about the injustice and unkindness of the world, that make Galsworthy such an attractive and dignified figure in spite of his limitation. But Bennett was a writer of far more genuine talent"[40]. Compared to other successful Edwardian writers he is less dependent on the idea that a moral is always necessary and that the writer should make the reader aware at every instant which side he is taking. Bennett is detached from the Victorians but, at the same time, he accepts the idea of omniscience precisely because he does not want the novel to represent the triumph of ambiguity, hermeneutic enigmas or exhausting psychological subtleties that are unappetizing to the common reader, but to be the expression of interesting daily lives that develops in time: Bennett's characters always have their eyes on the clock and it is this daily time with which they have to constantly deal. In this struggle between the individual and time, Bennett never attempts to simplify matters or take short cuts towards a monological definition of character. His protagonists are always captured in the process of becoming in their inevitable confrontation with the mysteries and enigmas of life. In this respect, David Lodge is right when in *The Modes of Modern Writing*, he considers Bennett as one of the greatest representatives of English realism. In particular, Lodge shows how Bennett shares a similar attitude of reticence to James, for in many of his works he transfers onto a visible plane (a scene, a colour or a series of sequences) what cannot be described because it does not correspond to the social codes or common sense of morality. Lodge explicitly points out, for example, how the scene of the capital punishment in Paris in *The Old Wives' Tale* is connected to sexuality

> [...] it is obvious that if Bennett, in the manner of a present-day novelist, had described the sexual side of the honeymoon in detail, it would have been as trauma

---

40   G. S. Fraser, *The Modern Writer and His World*, Harmondsworth, Penguin, 1972, p. 84.

for Sophia: everything we are told about her and Scales compels this deduction. The reticence of Edwardian taste, or Bennett's own reticence, led him to transfer this trauma to the execution (though without leaving the bedroom)[41].

It is precisely this reticence that establishes a certain significant distance between naturalism and Bennett's narrative method. In his avoidance of an exaggerated or hyperbolic representation of events, the writer opts for a measured approach, in which his conscious censorship of sexuality allows him to be linguistically in control of the text. One may even go so far as to say that his completely Edwardian reticence testifies to his relationship of continuity (even if limited to the sexual sphere) with the tradition of the Victorian novel. The question of reticence with regard to sexuality is not applicable, of course, to a writer like D. H. Lawrence who, although defined a modernist, adopts stylistic strategies that derive from Victorian realism rather than the modernism of Joyce. Lawrence's innovation lies in content rather than form because he does not follow the new paths of experimentation which would destabilise the novelistic form as conceived by F. R. Leavis's "great tradition"[42].

As appears evident, the question of the novel is one of representation: every writer elaborates a series of strategies in order that his or her ideas – and, by extension, literary imagination – may discover the most appropriate expression in terms of verbal representation. As is always the case with artistic products, the problem regards the awareness of the writer who, in search of their literary identity, will always have to reckon with a tradition they will at the same time attempt to transcend. Bennett knew very well that this was the artist's function. In fact, while he wrestled with the problem of transcending the great models of the past, he also felt an urgency to reach as many readers as possible with captivating stories which would enable them to discover a pleasure for reading. In this particular aspect, the Victorians had very clear ideas. Dickens was a case in point. For Bennett, Dickens was not so much the best artistic model to emulate as a novelist who had

---

41   David Lodge, *The Modes of Modern Writing*, London, Edward Arnold, 1977, p. 30.

42   F. R. Leavis, *The Great Tradition: George Eliot, Henry James, Joseph Conrad*, Harmondsworth and New York, Penguin, 1983.

understood the demands of the literary marketplace. It was Dickens who, with his journals, had invented a way of transforming his artistic talent into something that could be sold profitably. Yet Dickens was certainly not among the Victorian novelists Bennett admired the most. Indeed, he did not hesitate to criticise him for being devoid of a feeling for beauty and a feeling for literature. Thus, it is significant that in 1914 in *The Author's Craft*, Bennett specifically links Thackeray and Dickens in terms of their approach to reality and particularly asserts that "[Dickens] fell short in courageous facing of the truth, and in certain delicacies of perception"[43]. Ultimately, Bennett is drawn to the French, rather than the English novel which, at least in Thackeray and Dickens, seemed to him to be too misleading and superficial in its representation of the truth. This polemical attitude is a reflection of Bennett's refusal of every form of extremity – whether it be satire or an excessively exaggerated view of daily life – which explains why, among the many defects of which he accuses Dickens, there is also his "constant search for ugliness". In short, Bennett's most important model remained Fielding who, for him, possessed that "great quality of mind" that makes a great writer: "Fielding lives unequalled among English novelists because the broad nobility of his mind is unequalled. He is read with unreserved enthusiasm because the reader feels himself at each paragraph to be in close contact with a glorious personality"[44]. In a sense, it is precisely the same harmony, nobility and elegance of Fielding's representation of real life that Bennett seeks to achieve in his own novels[45].

---

43 Arnold Bennett, *The Author's Craft*, London, New York, George H. Doran, 1914, p. 47.

44 *Ibid.*, p. 46.

45 One writer of the nineteenth century whom Bennett praises and for whom he felt a sort of veneration during his formative years is Ouida: "The one author whom as a youth I 'devoured' was Ouida, creator of the incomparable Strathmore, the Strathmore upon whose wrath the sun unfortunately went down. I loved Ouida much for the impassionate nobility of her style, but more for the scene of gilded vice into which she introduced me". Arnold Bennett, *The Truth About an Author*, New York, George H. Doran, 1911, p. 20.

CHAPTER 2 Character formation and narrative ambiguity in *Anna of the Five Towns*

1. In spite of the fact that it is based exclusively on a female character – Anna Tellwright – *Anna of the Five Towns* is a novel in which the social context plays a role of the utmost importance. In fact, a complete interpretation of the work is impossible without taking into serious consideration the narrow confines of the socioeconomic and religious background against which the story unfolds[46]. The novel was published in September 1902 by Chatto and Windus. However, Bennett had begun working on it as far back as 1896, when, in a letter to George Sturt, he wrote: "I know a good lot about my second novel already – *mœurs de province* it will be, utterly unliterary"[47]. As is always the case in an epistolary discourse, Bennett's words must be read in light of his correspondent: Sturt had a passion for historical novels and considered Walter Scott to be one of the greatest figures of English literature, while at the same time he rejected the novelistic models coming from France. Clearly, therefore, the expression "utterly unliterary" also implies a kind of heroism that has little to do with Scott's characters or the world he deals with. The world Bennett has in mind is an industrial England of which he knows every detail down to the bone.

---

46 On the nature of Bennett's realism Warren Beach has commented: "His realism is of a mild, domestic variety somewhat suggestive of Howells, but rather more incisive, in which the most is made of minor events and vicissitudes of ordinary life among middle-class people – the conflict of wills in the family between parents and children, between sisters, and between married people". Joseph Warren Beach, *English Literature of the Nineteenth and the Early Twentieth Centuries – 1798 to the First World War*, New York, Collier Books, 1962, p. 241.

47 Hepburn, *op. cit.*, vol. II, p. 36. Henceforth all quotations are from this edition indicated in the text as *Letters* followed by the indication of the volume and page number. The letter is dated 18 February 1896. George Sturt was a man of letters and author of novels with whom Bennett had a long correspondence in spite of their completely different views on the novel. See Margaret Drabble, *op. cit.*, pp. 61–63.

As regards the genesis of the novel, Bennett was still undecided about the title when he finished writing it in May 1901. In March 1896 its title was *A Strange Woman*, which he changed six months later to *Sis Marigold*. However, he must have felt that the surname Marigold was too blatantly connotative of wealth, for two months later he changed the title again to *Sis Tellwright*, then to *Anna Tellwright*, before finally deciding on *Anna of the Five Towns*. It cannot go unnoticed that all of these titles have in common the fact that they refer to a female protagonist. Furthermore, Bennett's focus on the woman's role in the Potteries may be regarded as an early analysis of change through a heroine who is forced to endure events. In this sense, it would not be inappropriate to consider *Anna of the Five Towns* as an experimental anticipation of his more complex novel *The Old Wives' Tale*. As shall be seen, this novel places at the centre of the story the parallel destinies of two sisters who, in various ways, experience the cultural anxieties and social limitations of a world which refuses to abandon Victorian codes of morality.

Although the two novels are different in almost every aspect (characterisation, plot, social context and sentimental situation) the story of Anna Tellwright anticipates the atmosphere that characterises *The Old Wives' Tale*. In *Anna of the Five Towns* also, Methodism assumes particular importance. First and foremost, it is a form of continuity with the past and, in other respects, of behavioural codes and values in which women have become socially entrapped. For this reason, one of the dominant cultural features of the novel is its religious context in which is reflected the industriousness of the labourers and entrepreneurs of the Potteries and their obsession for accumulating money coupled with their negation of every form of pleasure[48].

---

48   It is no exaggeration to say that from the time John Wesley (1703–1791) was giving his first sermons, the industrial district of the Potteries was one of the strongholds of Methodism and could count on the support of some very influential porcelain manufacturers as Josiah Wedgwood and Enoch Wood for its development. Indeed, by the time Bennett was born, the Methodist tradition in Burslem was already well consolidated. Wesley's first visit dated back to 1760, when, thorough his sermons, he gained a great number of proselytes from different social levels. As biographers have noted, during the period from 1760 to 1785, Wesley visited the Potteries several times always obtaining consensus in what was an area of large demographic expansion – if Burslem counted only

In this respect, the diegesis of the novel is developed in terms of an essentially protestant ethic. As Max Weber has justly observed of industrial capitalism: "the statement that the fulfilment of worldly duties is under all circumstances the only way to live acceptably to God. It and it alone is the will of God, and hence every legitimate calling has exactly the same worth in the sight of God"[49]. Although Bennett is careful to avoid direct comment, he renders such an approach to the economic world with great efficacy throughout the novel. In addition, the protestant ethic urges individuals to work for the glory of God and refrain from spending their money on pleasurable things. Thus, in the absence of a business project, those who accumulate money are finally enslaved by it and transformed into misers or usurers.

The story at the centre of *Anna of the Five Towns* is also that of a father who denies his daughters, Anna and her younger sister Agnes, the right to live their own lives. In this sense, Drabble suggests seeing it as a *parent novel*:

> The parent novel is Balzac's *Eugénie Grandet*, also a novel of provincial life. It's revealing that Bennett even used the French phrase, *mœurs de province*, in sketching out his intentions to Sturt. Both novels have young girls as their central characters, but both young girls are overshadowed by their miser fathers. Eugénie and Anna are both wooed for their wealth, and both fall in love unsuitably; both defy their fathers for their loved ones, and defy him in financial terms, the only terms he understands – Eugénie gives away her birthday gold [...] to her worthless cousin Charles, and Anna burns a bill of exchange to prevent prosecution of Willie Price, a defaulting tenant[50].

7500 inhabitants in 1760, the number more than doubled in 1785 as can be seen by its commercial and industrial growth. On the proliferation of Methodism and Wesley's charisma and oratorical skills see J. H. Overton, *John Wesley*, London, Methuen, 1891; and John Pollock, *Wesley The Preacher*, Eastbourne, Kingsway Publications, 2003.

49   Max Weber, *The Protestant Ethic and the Spirito of Capitalism*, London and New York, Routledge, 2001, p. 41. See also Tawney: "Religion must be active, not merely contemplative. Contemplation is, indeed, a kind of self-indulgence [...] Covetousness is a danger to the soul, buti t is not so grave a danger as sloth". R. H. Tawney, *Religion and the Rise of Capitalism. A Historical Study*, with a prefatory note by Dr Charles Gore, Harmondsworth, Penguin, [1922, 1926], 1972, p. 241.

50   Drabble, *op. cit.*, p. 95.

Nevertheless, it would be incorrect to consider Bennett's novel as an English version of Balzac. As has been pointed out, the ethical and religious context and, generally, the society in which Anna Tellwright lives are completely different. It would be more appropriate to see Bennett, who was always alert to nineteenth-century French literature, consciously drawing on Balzac, fully aware that his work would be completely different. However, the fact that Bennett initially adopted the surname Mari*gold* does not exclude, with its reference to gold, the influence of *Eugénie Grandet*.

Nonetheless, composition on the novel was discontinuous. After conceiving the idea in September 1898, Bennett expressed his artistic dilemmas in his diary:

> My serious novel *Anne Tellwright* with which I have made some progress is put aside indefinitely – or rather until I have seen what I can do. To write popular fiction is offensive to me, but it is far more agreeable than being tied daily to an office and editing a lady's paper; and perhaps it is less ignoble, and less of a strain on the conscience. To edit a lady's paper, even a relatively advanced one, is to foster conventionality and hinder progress regularly once a week. Moreover I think that fiction will pay better, and in order to be happy I must have a fair supply of money[51].

Clearly, Bennett was aware of the extent to which *Anna of the Five Towns* would be a demanding novel to write. It would be based on the artistic world, which in this case meant literary research, the abandonment of any kind of facile sensationalism, a plot that would deal with daily life as closely as possible but also have to adopt narrative strategies which would be easily appreciated by the common reader. His slow progress can be explained by the fact that the novel would be very different from his earlier works which had been written exclusively for popular taste and financial profit. It is significant also that Bennet declares the writing of "popular fiction" to be offensive to his art, however preferable to writing articles or editing a lady's magazine. At the end of his note, however, he also deems that novel writing – even if not for popular taste – will allow him to earn money which will be fundamental for his personal happiness.

---

51   Arnold Bennett, *The Journals*, Harmondsworth, Penguin, 1971, p. 51.

This particular emphasis on money would have a powerful thematic relevance on *Anna of the Five Towns* given the fact that possession and lack of money are at the heart of the novel. As a result, although Bennett is associating wealth with happiness on a personal level, he is also already reflecting on the story of the heroine of *Anna of the Five Towns* precisely because, as shall be seen, money will be the source of salvation or despair for those who inspire Anna's affection.

Another aspect which has not been sufficiently underlined by critics concerns the sociological attention Bennett reserved for the historical and social structure in order to give substance to his idea of a "serious novel". In fact, although the writer himself had been born and bred in the Potteries and thus was quite familiar with its environment and the character of its people, he went back to the Five Towns in order to document its reality more accurately, convinced that this would help him emerge from his creative deadlock and provide new stimulus for his imagination not so much in sociological as visibly suggestive terms. The moment in which he made this decision can be seen in his *Journals* where, under the date 18 April 1899, his annotations throw an interesting light on the genesis of the novel:

> I finished the draft of *Anna Tellwright* just before Easter – having written it at the rate of eight or ten thousand words a week – and till that was done I had no leisure for keeping a journal or spare energies for observation. I went home at Easter in order to collect facts useful for the novel, and I got what I wanted. The novel however is to rest till after Whitsuntide[52].

Bennett refuses to consider his new novel as simply the product of a writer who is able to produce words at a rate that would be the envy of Trollope[53]. As he confesses, he can only proceed at a very slow pace, since to produce ten thousand words a week means little more than three

---

52   *Ibid.*, pp. 57–58.
53   Incidentally, the rate at which Trollope wrote suggests that his activity was only a question of quantity. Obviously, this was not the case: in spite of his workaholic method, his greatness is beyond question. As regards the number of words he produced daily, the Victorian novelist writes: "It had at this time become my custom [...] to write with my watch before me, and to require from myself 250 words every quarter of an hour. I have found that the 250 words have been forthcoming as regularly as my watch went". Anthony Trollope, *An Autobiography*,

or four pages a day. Moreover, it is significant that, once he acquired the necessary documentation[54], the writer took the decision not to start work on *Anna Tellwright* immediately in order to radically revise the text, but to dedicate himself to other literary activities such as writing articles for the journal *Academy* and some short stories. Only a few months later, at the beginning of November of the same year, would Bennett take up the manuscript again with the attitude of a writer who cannot be content to make any compromises with respect to his initial project. In this case also his diary provides some important insights:

> Yesterday and today I have been reading through the draft of *Anna Tellwright*. It came fresh to me. Some involutions of the plot I had quite forgotten. On the whole I was pleased with it. Much of it impressed me to a surprising extent, but the end will have to be approached more slowly; it needs to be "prepared"; and when it comes it must be described with much greater detail.
>
> I tried very hard to make a satisfactory beginning of the final writing of *Anna Tellwright* this afternoon, and could do absolutely nothing couldn't get a sentence that wasn't drivel[55].

Bennett's words are a testimony of the difficulties that his new novel was posing. At the same time, however, they reveal the strict approach of an author who, on re-reading the first draft, discovers a series of weak points which also concern the diegetic development of which he evidences "some involutions". He refers above all to the epilogue which, at this phase of composition, seems rushed and therefore not

---

  ed. Michael Sadleir and Frederick Page, Oxford, Oxford University Press, 1989, p. 272.

54 On his return to the Potteries and his brief stay at Burlem in 1897, Bennett tried to collect detailed information about Methodism and its importance for the population of the Five Towns as well as the buildings in which the faithful held their reunions. In any case, Bennett already had a clear idea of the area so that, in all probability, it had been his literary scruples that had led him there. On this point, it is worth reading what A. C. Judson wrote in 1923 about Bennett and the Potteries: "He knows the Five Towns with that intimacy which is a divine gift to youth alone [...] It is this knowledge, it seems to me, rather than any essential characteristics of the region or the people, that has made Bennett's Five Towns novels memorable". A. C. Judson, "Arnold Bennett and the Five Towns", *Texas Review*, 8, 2 (January 1923), p. 195.

55 Bennett, *The Journals*, cit., pp. 61–62.

very credible. However, the fact that the title of the novel is still *Anna Tellwright* confirms the importance of the heroine in Bennett's imagination. Only on further reflection would he decide to give more prominence to the topology of the novel thereby establishing a direct link between the protagonist and the place in which she lives, almost as if to sanction the fact that, besides being the heroine's natural space, the Five Towns define the perimeters of her imprisonment[56].

However, what emerges above all is the writer's almost obsessive preoccupation with the beginning and end of the story. Undoubtedly, his insistence on the importance of the beginning and the structuring of an adequate closure are the signs of an acute artistic awareness. His search for a sense of measure, a suitable atmosphere and, even more important, the right words to explain the indisputable success of *Anna of the Five Towns*.[57]. As seen in his diary, Bennett did not write the final words until 17 May 1901, "after 17 hours' continuous work, save for meals, on the last 5,000 words. I was very pleased with it"[58].

---

56   For an analysis of space as a metalinguistically relevant semiotic element see Francesco Marroni, "The Paradigm of Negativity in *Anna of the Five Towns*", *Cahiers Victoriens et Edouardiens*, 41 (avril 1995), pp. 99–120.

57   Harold Bloom, *The Western Canon*, New York, Riverhead Books, 1995, p. 522. While Bloom's list includes *The Old Wives' Tale*, it excludes *Anna of the Five Towns*. Bloom's may be an authoratative voice but it goes without saying that the English literary canoni is – like the literature of any other country – subject to revisions and reassessments. Besides, as far as *Anna of the Five Towns* is concerned, many critics are not of the same mind as Bloom. To quote one important example from the 1950s, Walter Allen considers the novel as part of the canon declaring that "the triumph of the novel is Anna, that compound of honesty, innocence, and pride who cannot bring herself to be publicly saved as the revival and who, in the greatest moment of her life, can flout her upbringing and defy her father from sheer compassion for Willie Price". Walter Allen, *The English Novel*, Harmondsworth, Penguin, 1984 [1954], pp. 320–321. In the same period, the American critic William York Tindall gave a very positive judgment of *Anna of the Five Towns*: "a serious study of a commonplace woman in the pottery district, a satire on Methodism and parental tyranny, and a firm re-creation of environment. [...] With this admirably restrained story of dullness and frustration Bennett found his subject and his manner". William York Tindall, *Forces in Modern British Literature 1885–1956*, New York, Vintage Books/Random House, 1956, p. 133.

58   Bennett, *The Journals*, cit., p. 67.

Bennett's satisfaction derives from the fact that he succeeded in finding the right balance between the private dimension of Anna's love story and the public dimension of the provincialism and moral blindness of the Potteries, Wesleyan Methodism fictionalised as a religious practice and way of life and a changing world in which few become rich and many remain in poverty. In *Anna of the Five Towns*, Bennett portrays everything with the utmost realism and avoids rigidly binding his narrative technique to the influence of naturalism. Ultimately, it is a work that bears the mark of the literary imagination of its author.

2. An analysis of the novel cannot escape a consideration of the religious coordinates which determine the thoughts and attitudes of the protagonist. In this context, Harvey has rightly observed that *"Anna of the Five Towns focuses on the economic and spiritual life of the industrial Midlands, drawing on Bennett's early immersion in Wesleyan Methodism which centered on the Sunday Schools that dominated the lives of so many of his contemporaries, his intimate knowledge of the working of a pot-bank, and his family holidays in the Isle of Man"*[59]. Behind the plot and the network of references to the industrial world of the Potteries, are autobiographical details from which Bennett derives a series of elements which make up the structure of the novel. From the very start the narrator aims to create an environment dominated by Methodism which, as has already been underlined, constitutes the sociological frame within which every action of all the characters can be explained. In Bennett's works, the incipit is always a moment of particular semantic and structural complexity perfectly functional to the development of the narrative[60]. In any event, the first page immediately introduces the reader to a world in which religious zeal is exercised in

---

[59]   Geoffrey M. Harvey, "Narrowing the Abyss: Arnold Bennett's *Anna of the Five Towns*", *Études Anglaises*, 60, 1 (2007), p. 31.

[60]   Mention must be made here of what Hillis Miller says regarding the importance of the beginning of novels as well as of works of any other literary genre: "For me the opening sentences of literary works have special force. They are 'Open Sesames' unlocking the door to that particular work's fictive realm. All it takes is a few words, and I become a believer, a seer. I become the fascinated witness of a new virtual reality". J. Hillis Miller, *On Literature: Thinking in Action*, London and New York, Routledge, 2002, p. 24.

the Sunday Schools which were so important for the spiritual formation of the individual and the Methodist faith:

> The yard was all silent and empty under the burning afternoon heat, which had made its asphalt springy like turf, when suddenly the children threw themselves out of the great doors at either end of the Sunday-school – boys from the right, girls from the left – in two howling, impetuous streams, that widened, eddied, inter-mingled, and formed backwaters until the whole quadrangle was full of clamour and movement. [...] Near the left-hand door a little girl of twelve years, dressed in a cream coloured frock, with a wide and heavy straw hat, stood quietly kicking her foal-like legs against the wall. She was one of those who had won a prize, and once or twice she took the treasure from under her arm to glance at its frontispiece with a vague smile of satisfaction. For a time her bright eyes were fixed expectantly on the doorway; then they would wander, and she started to count the windows of the various Connexional buildings which on three sides enclosed the yard – chapel, school, lecture-hall, and chapel-keeper's house[61].

The description of the children rushing out from the Sunday-school serves to establish the direct link in the novel between scholastic education and religious formation and their influence on the psychology and behaviour of its characters. Indeed, it is immediately apparent that, from a narratolo-gical point of view, the context assumes a particular relevance with regard to the characters, including the heroine, who, as one of the Sunday-School teachers, is the last to enter the scene. The initial focus is on Anna's little sister, Agnes, who is silently exulting over her school-prize. But no sooner is she introduced than the narrator draws attention to the spatial dimension which, as always in Bennett, will be of utmost importance to the novel.

The reference to the Methodist "connexional buildings" may appear rather cryptic to a common reader. The term *connexion* seems to refer to a sort of congregation, but even this inference does not tell us much about the nature of Methodist worship. The origin of the term dates back to 1797[62], six months after the death of its founder John

---

61   Arnold Bennett, *Anna of the Five Towns*, Introduction by Frank Swinnerton, London, Penguin, 2001, p. 15. Henceforth, all quotations refer to this edition and are indicated in the text as *AFT* followed by the page number.

62   On this topic see "The city of Stoke-on-Trent: Protestant Nonconformity", in *A History of the County of Stafford: Volume 8*, ed. J. G. Jenkins (London, 1963), pp. 276–307. *British History Online* http://www.british-history.ac.uk/vch/staffs/vol8/pp276-307 [last access 26 August 2016]. "[i]n July 1797, when the annual

Wesley, when a group of Methodists in the area of the Potteries, split from the main body of Methodists because they did not recognise the religious practices that were introduced after Wesley's death. This new group went by the name of the "Methodist New Connexion" and to distinguish themselves from the original Methodists, they adopted the adjective *connexional* to define what they regarded as their more enlightened form of Methodism which refuted the more fundamentalist approach[63].

Besides Bennett's use of this very local religious term, the most striking aspect of the opening pages is the extent to which all of the characters are directly involved in Methodism which is immediately presented as a deeply rooted factor of the everyday life of the Five Towns. It is precisely while she is waiting for her sister that Agnes recognises two young men of the "New Connexion":

> She looked round with a jump, and blushed, smiling and screwing up her little shoulders, when she recognised the two men who were coming towards her from the door of the lecture-hall. The one who had called out was Henry Mynors, morning superintendent of the Sunday-school and conductor of the men's Bible-class held in the lecture-hall on Sunday afternoons. The other was William

---

conference of the Methodist Church was held at Leeds, there were five Methodist chapels in the Potteries, at Longton, Fenton, Hanley, Burslem, and Tunstall, and a regular meeting at Stoke. Support for the Kilhamite demands, the rejection of which at this conference resulted in the formation of the Methodist New Itinerancy or Connexion, had already been shown by the members of Hanley chapel and this had resulted in the temporary closing of the chapel by the trustees. By September 1797, less than two months after the formation of the Methodist New Connexion, there were five societies of this church in the Potteries, at Hanley, Burslem, Longton, Sneyd Green, and Etruria. Hanley Wesleyan Methodist society was almost extinguished by the New Connexion group there, while Fenton chapel went over to the New Connexion".

63   It may be useful to recall that the term "Methodism" has connotations with fanaticism in that its origin goes back to the idea of applying the teachings of the Bible with method, that is, a precise and scrupulous adherence to the words of Holy Scripture. As Tomkins writes: "For almost as long as he had preached faith, Wesley had preached perfection. He passionately believed that the Bible promised the Christian life could be free from sin". Stephen Tomkins, *John Wesley: A Biography*, London, Lion Publishing, 2003, p. 156.

Price, usually styled Willie Price, secretary of the same Bible- class, and son of Titus Price, the afternoon superintendent (*AFT*, p. 16).

This passage introduces the two male protagonists who will play such crucial roles in the sentimental life of the heroine; Henry Mynors e Willie Price. The first is the champion of a society who believes that success and money are an expression of God's blessing. The second, who has also based his life around the same religious faith, is unable to believe that the grave financial problems that have inflicted his family can be a direct sign of divine will. Although they share the same ideological space, Henry Mynors and Willie Price represent contrasting attitudes which will never be reconciled, even by the strict adherence to the same faith.

Mynors represents a social 'perfection' which somewhat mystifies Agnes: "[...] she thought how perfect a man Mr. Mynors was [...] that mysterious, delicious, inexpressible something which dwelt behind his eyes: these constituted an ideal for her" (*AFT*, p. 16). Against Mynors' 'perfection' is the imperfection of the twenty-one-year-old Price, who, besides being nine years his junior, is also his social inferior. As a result, Price is never at his ease and his movements reveals a nature that is "sheepish and self-conscious" (*AFT*, p. 17). This temperament foreshadows the tragedy of those who are on the side of the defeated in society and compelled to pay the price for their condition of inferiority. If Mynors exudes the confidence and joviality of a man who is easily able to win the favour of Anna's little sister, Willie Price expresses the anxiety of a man who feels the earth moving under his feet.

Thus, from the opening pages of *Anna of the Five Towns* are made apparent the terms of conflict in the Potteries, of a world in which there are no intermediary spaces or points of connection. On a social and psychological level, one is either on the side of the victors or the defeated. No other form of mediation is possible. It must also be noticed that the first chapter is titled "The Kindling of Love", thus conveying the idea of a love story in which two men are competing against each other, even if not on equal terms. For what are the carefree and audacious Henry Mynors and the awkward and almost aphasic Willie Price doing outside a Methodist Sunday-school on a Sunday afternoon if they are not – like the little Agnes – waiting for Anna to arrive?

As John Lucas has justly observed: "Both of them are potters, Mynors successful, Willie, because of his father's incompetence, on the verge of failure. As a successful potter, Mynors is socially important. [...] It is a point we need to remember when we find that Anna is flattered by his paying her attentions. And it is an indication of her necessarily limited vision that she should see him as a glamorous figure, just as it is an indication of Bennett's adroit and scrupulous handling of social gradations that Mynors should seem much more attractive and worldly to Anna than Willie Price does"[64]. In view of the series of relations described (Henry Mynors *vs.* Willie Price, success *vs.* failure, sympathy *vs.* reticence, words *vs.* silence), the description of the heroine presents a series of unmistakable interconnections:

> Anna Tellwright stood motionless for a second in the shadow of the doorway. She was tall, but not unusually so, and sturdily built up. Her figure, though the bust was a little flat, had the lenient curves of absolute maturity. Anna had been a woman since seventeen, and she was now on the eve of her twenty-first birthday. She wore a plain, home-made light frock checked with brown and edged with brown velvet, thin cotton gloves of cream colour, and a broad straw hat like her sister's. Her grave face, owing to the prominence of the cheekbones and the width of the jaw, had a slight angularity; the lips were thin, the brown eyes rather large, the eyebrows level, the nose fine and delicate; the ears could scarcely be seen for the dark brown hair which was brushed diagonally across the temples, leaving of the forehead only a pale triangle. It seemed a face for the cloister, austere in contour, fervent in expression, the severity of it mollified by that resigned and spiritual melancholy peculiar to women who, through the error of destiny, have been born into a wrong environment (*AFT*, p. 19).

---

64   John Lucas, *Arnold Bennett: A Study of his Fiction*, London, Methuen, 1974, p. 42. On the contrast between Henry Mynors and Willie Price, Elizabeth Jones evidences the inevitability of Price's suicide: "Throughout the novel we follow Mynors from success to success, while in contrast, as a direct result of the failure of his industry, we witness Willie Price's life come crashing down around him. His debt, his illegal forgery, his father's suicide, the loss of his business and his family home, the death of his housekeeper and finally Anna's decision to marry Mynors, ultimately leaves him nothing to live for, pushing him towards the tragic resolution of suicide". Elizabeth Jones, "Work and Industry in *Anna of the Five Towns*", *Innervate*, vol. 2 (2009–2010), p. 259. https://www.nottingham.ac.uk/english/documents/innervate/09-10/0910jon eseworkindustry.pdf [last accessed 27 August 2016].

The description is typical of Bennett's tendency to present physical features as a way of defining more acutely the internal attributes of a character. Thus, the initial impression of immobility is subsequently linked to the final reference to the cloister: Anna Tellwright resembles a nun whose expression gives the onlooker the impression of fervour, melancholy and austerity. These three characteristics correspond to the three aspects of her personality: the religious fervour in which she has been educated: her underlying melancholy and the severity that is the dominant element of a society accustomed to judging people according to the strict codes passed down by non-conformist tradition.

These three semantic fields seem to be further reinforced by her angular physiognomy[65] ("a slight angularity" and "a pale triangle") which seems in syntony with the harsh life of the Potteries. It is easy to conclude that the description of Anna's face closely connects immobility with the idea of non-life. In this particular case, death is not simply social death, but also the death of the person whom she feels she loves but whom she cannot love because of her inability to be herself and act with self-assertion.

Besides, the fact that she feels in conflict with her hometown means that, in her case, "the error of destiny" also calls into question its ontological dimension. Since she remains closed within the hard shell of the privacy of her daily life, Anna appears to everyone to be different to the way she really is and, consequently, is misunderstood by everyone in the community: "She had no friends; her innate reserve had been misinterpreted, and she was not popular among the Wesleyan community" (*AFT*, p. 23). The opening scene in which she appears alone at the school entrance while her sister is waiting for her is indicative of her lack of sociability and loneliness. Meanwhile her hard inner self which knows nothing of the exhilaration of love is shaken by the presence of her two suitors who, in some way, provide a moment of excitement and self- esteem. For while it is true that Henry Mynors is courting the

---

65   As Barthes recalls, angularity – in other words, non-softness of lines – is associated with the idea of death. As the French critic writes: death is evoked in a "signified which connotes angularity, geometry, the broken line, a form antithetic of vapour and vegetable, that is life" Roland Barthes, *S/Z*, Torino, Einaudi, 1973, p. 36.

heroine because he knows very well that her father, being the miser he is, has hoarded a great sum of money over the years, Willie Price is attracted by her temperament and her shyness, because it seems to him to reflect his own. Consequently, a dialogue is established between the two young people in which silence is more important than words. Mynors, on the contrary, arouses contrasting feelings in Anna:

> [...] his attitude had even enabled her in a few moments to establish a pleasant familiarity with him. Nevertheless, as they joined the stream of people in Moor Road, she longed to be at home, in her kitchen, in order to examine herself and the new situation thus created by Mynors. And yet also she was glad that she must remain at his side, but it was a fluttered joy that his presence gave her, too strange for immediate appreciation. As her eye, without directly looking at him, embraced the suave and admirable male creature within its field of vision, she became aware that he was quite inscrutable to her. What were his inmost thoughts, his ideals, the histories of his heart? Surely it was impossible that she should ever know these secrets! He – and she: they were utterly foreign to each other (*AFT*, p. 22).

Anna's inner confusion is combined here with her fear that she will not be able to share her future with such a confident and popular man as Mynors. It also appears symptomatic that she would rather be in the private sphere of her kitchen where she can be alone with herself to think about her life and her feelings concerning her future prospects as a woman, than walking along the bustling streets of the town.

At the same time, it cannot go unnoticed that the familiarity established with Mynors is not the result of a deep attachment. This is confirmed by the words of the omniscient narrator who later declares that, all things considered, Anna and Mynors are two strangers from two different worlds: "What were his inmost thoughts, his ideals, the histories of his heart? Surely it was impossible that she should ever know these secrets!". Mynors' world is shrouded in secret and Anna wonders what her suitor's thoughts and ideals could be precisely because, in spite of his talkative and pleasant nature, he remains a mystery to her.

3. Anna's sole point of reference is undoubtedly her kitchen. In her world-view, it represents continuity against the painful conflicts and discontinuity of her society. It is no accident, therefore, that the private space of her kitchen – her authentic *locus* of liberty and independence – becomes a form of self-defence against the mysterious valency

characterising Mynors. David Ormerod has justly underlined the importance of this domestic space: "The kitchen, in short, is a shrine, and Anna its votaress"[66]. Indeed, the narrator's description of Anna's kitchen highlights most explicitly this aspect of the place in terms of its ontological implications:

> Anna's kitchen was the only satisfactory apartment in the house. Its furniture included a dresser of the simple and dignified kind which is now assiduously collected by amateurs of old oak. It had four long narrow shelves holding plates and saucers; the cups were hung in a row on small brass hooks screwed into the fronts of the shelves. Below the shelves were three drawers in a line, with brass handles, and below the drawers was a large recess which held stone jars, a copper preserving-saucepan, and other receptacles. Seventy years of continuous polishing by a dynasty of priestesses of cleanliness had given to this dresser a rich ripe tone which the cleverest trade-trickster could not have imitated. In it was reflected the conscientious labour of generations. It had a soft and assuaged appearance, as though it had never been new and could never have been new. All its corners and edges had long lost the asperities of manufacture, and its smooth surfaces were marked by slight hollows similar in spirit to those worn by the naked feet of pilgrims into the marble steps of a shrine (*AFT*, pp. 105–106).

The meticulous description of the kitchen is not an end in itself but entirely relevant to the antiheroic fictionalisation of the protagonist herself. Every single element has a relevance which sets in motion a series of clues whose meaning is connected with Anna's lifetime. As the narrator explains, immediately after her mother's death, when she was only five years-old, Anna has used and cleaned these objects which, for about twenty years, have become part of her character and the sentimental signs of her personality, almost as if the drawers, plates and cups have acquired a life of their own and have established a silent form of communication with her.

Nevertheless, the description goes beyond this level. For the narrator also specifies the chronological dimension of the objects in the kitchen when he refers to the "[S]eventy years of continuous polishing by a dynasty of priestesses of cleanliness" In this sense, Anna is not simply the daughter of Ephraim Tellwright. She also belongs to a

---

66   David Ormerod, "Doorway and Windowframe: Aestheticism and the Iconography of Bennett's *Anna of the Five Towns*", *English Studies*, 2 (1997), p. 131.

genealogical line of women who have been deluded into thinking they have accomplished themselves within this space. In fact, it is impossible to fully comprehend the behavioural codes which determine Anna's choices in the daily life of the Potteries without taking into account their cultural roots. For Anna has also absorbed the idea of subordinance to the male figure of the household from this dynasty of women and, like them, has never questioned male authority and dominance. In this respect, she not only inherits the objects but also the thoughts and beliefs of all the women of the Tellwright family whose dominion in the household – as the narrator ironically suggests – has been a question of keeping everything clean and tidy.

The kitchen is described as a sacred place, a temple whose edges have been smoothed down by the hands of pilgrims. If the outside world is aggressive, rough and potentially deathly, Anna's kitchen, with its "smooth surfaces", suggests a place in which affection is still possible. The religious connotations (*priestesses, pilgrims, shrine*) contribute further to determine the coordinates of this conflict between external reality and Anna's domestic space. It is no accident that she is often compared to a nun who can only be herself within the narrow confines of her cell and the silence of the cloister.

Although he avoids using a sociological and propagandistic tone and is careful to represent rather than explain each situation, in *Anna of the Five Towns* Bennett dramatizes the customs and socio-cultural codes of a world still essentially based on the patriarchal values of Victorian society. Thus, the natural place for a woman to express her personality is her home, in which serenity, order and joy must reign supreme. Man, on the other hand, must face an aggressive, harsh and ruthless society and struggle daily to ensure that the woman is unharmed and uncontaminated by the destructive activity of competition for power and the conservation of one's social position. The representation of the Five Towns, therefore, still follows this Victorian paradigm.[67] – Anna

---

67   On the role of women in terms of extreme spatial restriction see Deirdre David, *Intellectual Women and Victorian Patriarchy*, Ithaca, NY, Cornell University Press, 1987. It may be interesting to remember here that the American scholar is prompted by the famous and oft quoted reply by Robert Southey, who was then poet laureate, to the young Charlotte Brontë: "Literature cannot be the business of a woman's life, and it ought not to be. The more she is engaged in

is the victim of this conception of gender: being a woman means being limited in one's movements while being a man means not to have limits and to be able to challenge and fight others without territorial or moral restrictions. For this reason, whenever Anna thinks about the world of the Potteries, she feels that outside her own home lie only destruction and death. On the other hand, whenever the narrator mentions material objects, above all the kitchen, he conveys a sense of continuity to the reader. As David Ormerod notes: "The further itemizing of the elements of Anna's kitchen – polished mustard tins, grandfather clock, Windsor chair, tile, list hearthrug – completes the impression of pre-industrial ethical profundity analogous to that advocated by William Morris in *News from Nowhere*"[68]. In other words, in line with nineteenth-century paradigms, Bennett describes a kitchen which looks back to the past precisely because "[it] had the humanized air of use and occupation which nothing but use and occupation can impart to senseless objects" (*AFT*, p, 107)[69]. In many ways, the humanised aspect of the kitchen reflects a society that is not yet totally industrialised. This is the world of the beginning of the nineteenth century in which

---

her proper duties, the less leisure will she have for it, even as an accomplishment and a recreation". (The letter is quoted by David in the "Preface", p. vii). In brief, domestic space (in the first place the kitchen) is where women must show their talent and not in literature or other 'masculine' activities.

68   Ormerod, *op. cit.*, p. 131.
69   It seems rather strange that Bennett's contemporaries were not sufficiently artistically sensitive to understand the functional valence of the description of the kitchen in the novel. For example, George Sturt, in a letter dated 15 September 1902, observes: "You make an inventory of the furniture in Anna's kitchen: you even interrupt for that purpose an interview which obviously was of a most crucial nature. But while you give three pages to the inventory, you can spare less than a page to the interview, and when it is over, the reader feels dished, because something must have happened – some interchange of emotion between Mynors and Anna – which you have said nothing about. Were those trivial sentences which they exchanged really all? Or if not, was it worthwhile to spend so much time in describing the colour of the oak dresser that you had no space left even for the colour of Anna's face or whatever might manifest her feelings at the time? [...] the kitchen details produce an atmosphere of hum-drum domestic life, continuous through years – not an atmosphere of excitement and thrill and impeding change", (*Letters*, vol. II, pp. 172–173).

the Potteries responded to John Wesley's powerful sermons during the first wave of Methodism and turned the area into such a stronghold of the religious movement[70].

Significantly, the description of the kitchen is much more than a naturalistic given for Bennett or an inventory of objects. To George Sturt, who reproached him for having blocked the flow of the narrative in lingering too much on that environment, Bennett replied curtly that he understood very little of the artistic value of the detailed representation of the objects concerned: "[...] your taste in imaginative work is crude & unreliable. I don't believe you have any genuine critical standard"[71].

On the level of the function of the text, there is another element that must be mentioned. Tellwright's house is not just any house since his life is connected to the local and national events of Methodism the beliefs and precepts of which have, in a certain sense, imbued the walls of every room and consequently conditioned the thoughts, choices and attitudes of all of the Tellwright inhabitants. It is no accident that Ephraim had an important and prestigious role as treasurer of the Methodist Society during the years in which he was fond of showing the elders and the faithful how he put all of his effort into the religious cause:

> She recalled the surprising dexterity with which he [Ephraim Tellwright] counted the coins, the peculiar smell of the bags, and her mother's bland exclamation, "Eh, Ephraim!" Tellwright belonged by birth to the Old Guard of Methodism; there was in his family a tradition of holy valour for the pure doctrine: his father, a Bursley man, had fought in the fight which preceded the famous Primitive Methodist Secession of 1808 at Bursley [...] As for Ephraim, he expounded the mystery of the Atonement in village conventicles and grew garrulous with God at prayer-meetings in the big Bethesda chapel; but he did these things as routine, without skill and without enthusiasm, because they gave him an unassailable

---

70   Wesley visited the Potteries for the first time in 1760, stopping at Burslem. "Wesley first preached in Newcastle-upon-Lyme as early as 1738, the year of his conversion. However, his first visit to Stoke-on-Trent was on 8 March 1760 when he spoke at a large meeting in Burslem. He often visited the town where the first Methodist society in the country was formed at Swan Bank Methodist Church after earlier visits to meeting in Bristol by Potteries coal miners". J. Keith Cheetham, *On the Trail of John Wesley*, Edinburgh, Luath Press, 2003, p. 113.

71   *Letters*, vol. II, p. 175.

position within the central group of the society. He was not, in fact, much smitten with either the doctrinal or the spiritual side of Methodism (*AFT*, pp. 31–32)[72].

Anna's behaviour can only be understood by taking into account the scenes which symbolically trace the course of her destiny. In particular, the scene in which her father, as treasurer of the congregation shows his wife and daughter his money-filled bags, reveals how in the mind of the little Anna a deeply symbolic image is implanted in which her father embodies the inextricable link between the possession of material wealth and religious faith. Bennett exposes the negative valence of the behavioural and moral codes represented by Tellwright which Anna has been brought up to accept as positive values. As the narrator ironically, and even scornfully remarks: "To him the circuit was a 'going concern', and he kept it in motion, serving the Lord in committee and over statements of account. The minister by his pleading might bring sinners to the penitent form, but it was Ephraim Tellwright who reduced the cost per head of souls saved, and so widened the frontiers of the Kingdom of Heaven" (*AFT*, p. 32). In a sense, the narrator is telling us that Tellright has always been a miser and that his fondness for money is superior to his Methodist faith. Moreover, his desire to save money is apparently superior to his desire to earn a place in Heaven.

This finds theological confirmation in the idea that God always rewards his most faithful servants with material wealth. From this point of view, Tellwright's attitude comes as no surprise, especially if one

---

72   From Ephraim Tellwright's first appearance in the novel, the narrator shows the pertinacity of his desire to accumulate wealth both through financial speculation and his marriage to a rich woman. What particularly emerges in the description is the mystery that surrounds his person and characterises his behaviour: "Ephraim Tellwright was one of the most extraordinary and most mysterious men in the Five Towns. The outer facts of his career were known to all, for his riches made him notorious; but the secret and intimate man none knew anything except Anna, and what little Anna knew had come to her by divination rather than discernment. A native of Hanbridge, he had inherited a small fortune from his father, who was a prominent Wesleyan Methodist. At thirty, owing mainly to investment in property which his calling of potter's valuer had helped him to choose with advantage, he was worth twenty thousand pounds, and he lived in lodgings on a total expenditure of about a hundred year" (*AFT*, pp. 30–31).

takes into account what Weber observes: "The greater the possessions the heavier, if the ascetic attitude toward life stands the test, the feeling of responsibility for them, for holding them undiminished for the glory of God and increasing them by restless effort"[73]. Thus, it is not important for Anna's father to be engaged in the practice of piety as such than to be given daily confirmation that the fact that his money is increasing means that he is on the right side. Tellwright's home is exclusively governed by the laws of material wealth which never forgive those who fail since their lack of success is a sign of unworthiness and therefore a sin in the eyes of God

As a consequence of this conception of communal life, Anna establishes a love-hate relationship with her father whose greed for money also implies closure towards others together with the firm negation of any form of altruism: "In the dissolving views of her own past, from which the rigour and pain seemed to have mysteriously departed, the chief figure was always her father – that sinister and formidable individuality, whom her mind hated but her heart disobediently loved" (*AFT*, p. 30). Anna realises that her hatred of her tyrannical father derives from the numerous acts of humiliation and frustrating prohibitions that the miser has inflicted on her. At the same time, the miser is also her father whom her heart tells her she must love as one should love those who have given us life. A father who, at times, is capable of being good with his daughters and who, at certain moments, shows a more human, sensitive side to his nature when he decides to be more sociable with others.

Although it occurs on an unconscious level, Ephraim Tellwright becomes the very model the heroine, conditioned by the religious and socioeconomic world of the Potteries, ends up seeking in her suitors. Whatever the case, we may conclude that the man of her choice is hardened to the axiological criteria she has absorbed during years of acceptation of her strict father's obstinately tyrannical behaviour. In this respect, Anna certainly does not see Willie Price as a figure who represents the security she desires. On the other hand, Henry Mynors appears to embody the emotional stability and economic security that her heart and mind are seeking in the man she must marry:

---

73   Weber, *op. cit.*, pp. 114–115.

He was standing up, the ends of his fingers pressed against the top of the table. Very carefully dressed as usual, he wore a brilliant new red necktie, and a gardenia in his button-hole. He seemed happy, wholesome, earnest, and unaffected. He had the elasticity of youth with the firm wisdom of age. And it was as if he had never been younger and would never grow older, remaining always at just thirty and in his prime. Incomparable to the rest, he was clearly born to lead. He fulfilled his functions with tact, grace, and dignity. In such an affair as this present he disclosed the attributes of the skilled workman, whose easy and exact movements are a joy and wonder to the beholder. And behind all was the man, his excellent and strong nature, his kindliness, his sincerity. Yes, to Anna, Mynors was perfect that night; the reality of him exceeded her dreamy meditations (*AFT*, pp. 56–57).

Although Anna's love for her father is dictated by her heart, her reason has the upper hand since it is forced to weigh all the indignities and limitations that he has made her suffer and continues to make her suffer even after she has reached the age of twenty-one. On the other hand, her decision to love Henry Mynors is not dictated by her heart, but is the result of a rational choice. In the description above, therefore, all of the lexemes which characterise Mynors, appeal to her rationality and need to feel protected and admired by a man of success: *happy, wholesome, earnest, unaffected*. The following lexemes and syntagms are also functional to such a portrait: *he was clearly born to lead, tact, grace, dignity, excellent and strong nature, his kindliness, his sincerity.* These words reflect a rational evaluation of the advantages and disadvantages before marriage by a woman who will consequently become a faithful and attentive wife. Nevertheless, there are no indications in Anna of the transportations of a woman in love who desires to be embraced by the man she admires. Her exaltation is not a sign of her love but the magnetic and powerful effect of Henry Mynors' presence. As a young successful Methodist, Mynors represents the social norm for a girl condemned to be isolated and shunned by everybody because she is seen by the community as the daughter of a miser, a speculator and tyrant.

4. Undoubtedly the tragic story of Willie Price's family constitutes precisely what the strict judgment of the Methodists considers as a divine condemnation. On a diegetic level, the first phase of this condemnation comes with the suicide of Titus Price, who hangs himself to avoid facing the dishonour of social ostracism and poverty. In

the second, and even more dramatic phase, is the choice made by Willie who, after deciding to leave for Australia, opts for a drastic and definitive solution to his conflicting emotions by throwing himself into an "abandoned pitshaft" (*AFT*, p. 236) in the attempt to drown himself and the sins of his family.

Symbolically, by concealing his suicide from the community and imagining that nobody will ever discover his corpse at the bottom of a well, Willie Price performs an extreme symbolic gesture of love towards Anna who continues to live under the illusion that he has begun a new life in a distant country and erased the shame and dishonour of his family and found success in Australia where, at the beginning of the twentieth century, Methodism counted many followers. From a narratological viewpoint, nobody in the Potteries knows anything about his tragic end except the narrator who – with the benefit of omniscience[74] – indirectly reveals to the reader at the end of the novel precisely what has happened:

> She had sucked in with her mother's milk the profound truth that a woman's life is always a renunciation, greater or less. Hers by chance was greater. Facing the future calmly and genially, she took oath with herself to be a good wife to the man whom, with all his excellences, she had never loved. Her thoughts often dwelt lovingly on Willie Price, whom she deemed to be pursuing in Australia an honourable and successful career, quickened at the outset by her hundred pounds. This vision of him was her stay. But neither she nor anyone in the Five Towns or elsewhere ever heard of Willie Price again. And well might none hear! The abandoned pitshaft does not deliver up its secret. And so – the Bank of

---

74   Wolfgang Iser, in the chapter "The Blank as a Potential Connection" of *The Act of Reading*, observes how a *blank* presupposes the possibility of establishing a connection during the reading phase. In the case of *Anna of the Five Towns* there is a narrative blank regarding the destiny of Willie Price which is only explained in the final lines of the novel. This is an example of the technique of literary indeterminacy: "What we have called the blank arises out of the indeterminacy of the text [...] the blank, however, designates a vacancy in the overall system of the text, the filling of which brings about an interaction of textual patterns. In other words, the need for completion is replaced here by the need for combination. It is only when the schemata of the text are related to one another that the imaginary object can begin to be formed, and it is the blanks that get this connecting operation under way". Wolfgang Iser, *The Act of Reading. A Theory of Aesthetic Response*, Baltimore and London, Johns Hopkins University Press, 1991, p. 182.

> England is the richer by a hundred pounds unclaimed, and the world the poorer by a simple and meek soul stung to revolt only in its last hour (*AFT*, pp. 235–236).

The final scene of the novel makes it clear that Anna is a figure of silence and renunciation not only because she is assigned this role by her society but also for what she has inherited from the generations of women in the same kitchen and the same environment whose lives have been a story of total subjection to men and total self-denial. It is no accident that when, on her twenty-first birthday, Anna learns she has inherited a fortune from her mother which has been deposited in a bank, she does not pose the problem of how to manage her money. Moreover, her father, on his part, does not even consider giving his daughter what is hers by law. He simply informs her that he will manage the enormous sum she has inherited and Anna passively agrees. On retrospect it is therefore easy to conclude that the love story is interwoven with a story in which money and business are what really count.

As Andrew Popp has observed, nothing is simple in the world of Anna Tellwright precisely because of this inextricable connection between sentiments and business, between the tension of the individual and the desire to possess more and more money. From an ontological and sentimental point of view, therefore, Anna's is the story of a human failure:

> As its title suggests, the novel concentrates on Anna Tellwright, taking in her relationship with her father, Ephraim, her religious faith and, in particular, her romance with Henry Mynors, a young potter manufacturer. Her relationship with Mynors is complex; she becomes first a partner in his extremely successful business and eventually his fiancé and then wife, though the extent to which she loves him remains ambiguous[75].

Obviously, the measure of Anna's love for Mynors cannot be quantified simply because her feelings cannot be calculated like money or property. The ambiguity lies exclusively in the fact that she does not love Henry Mynors for what he represents internally, but only for what the

---

75   Andrew Popp, " 'Though it is but a Promise': Business Probity in Arnold Bennett's *Anna of the Five Towns*", *Business History*, 48, 3 (July 2006), p. 334.

young Methodist entrepreneur is for the society of the Potteries: she is fascinated by the success and power he embodies, not the man himself.

Willie Price, on the other hand, whom Anna always associates with the idea of meekness, belongs to a completely different sphere. Interestingly, *meek* is also the adjective which the narrator uses in the closing sentence of the novel. Anna also uses the same adjective which she quotes from the Testament[76]:

> His tone was so earnest, so pathetic, that tears of compassion almost rose to her eyes as she looked at those simple naïve blue eyes of his. His lanky figure and clumsily-fitting clothes, his feeble placatory smile, the twitching movements of his long red hands, all contributed to the effect of his defencelessness. She thought of the test: *'Blessed are the meek'*, and saw in a flash the deep truth of it. Here were she and her father, rich, powerful, autocratic; and there were Willie Price and his father, commercial hares hunted by hounds of creditors, hares that turned in plaintive appeal to those greedy jaws for mercy. And yet, she, a hound, envied at that moment the hares. *Blessed are the meek*, blessed are the failures, blessed are the stupid, for they, unknown to themselves, have a grace which is denied to the haughty, the successful, and the wise (*AFT*, p. 88, corsivi miei).

The parallelism Anna establishes in her mind configures the contrasting position of two families which both live and practice the Methodist faith in the Potteries. The quotation from the Gospel According to Matthew, being an indirect anticipation of the final words of the novel (those referring to Willie Price) are a reminder to the reader of the profoundly religious culture concealed behind the figure of the protagonist. However, in spite of Methodism and the strong commitment of the family in practicing the faith, Ephraim Tellwright knows no pardon for those who err, especially the Price family which should have been among the best members of society precisely because they have played such an important role in the religious community.

Behind the negative judgement against the two "commercial hares" hounded by a group of creditors, is the Calvinist idea which sees lack of success in the world (and thus also in entrepreneurial activity) as deserving of divine punishment. The commonly accepted belief among the congregation is that the weak people who are left behind in

---

76   The quotation is from Matthew 5, 5: "Blessed are the meek: for they shall inherit the earth".

society are removed from God's protection and, as a result, must pay a price. During an encounter with Willie, Anna, who feels in conflict with this attitude, suddenly undergoes an epiphany which opens her eyes to Price's unfortunate destiny: *"'Blessed are the meek'*, and saw in a flash the deep truth of it"[77]. Suddenly, the heroine understands that it is not God that is persecuting Willie, but a society in which the weak have no place. She has a Darwinian realisation that the world of industry and commerce is a stage upon which a daily struggle for existence takes place. In this *struggle for life*, the weak are condemned to surrender and Willie Price belongs precisely to this category of person. The image of a hare chased by ravenous hounds gives an idea of the measure of this awareness since the heroine's imagination – even though unconsciously – draws precisely on Darwinian terminology in discussing the animal world in the oppositional terms of victim and executioner. In fact, Anna realises she is on the side of the executioners but being a woman without autonomy of thought, that is, being a heroine without quality, she can offer no alternative to the man she feels she loves[78], besides giving him a sum of money to facilitate his attempt in starting a new life in Australia.

In Bennett's representation of the Potteries there is no place for mercy or human understanding. The daily life of the Methodist

---

77 It may be noticed that Bennett provides the reader with a series of clues to understand what Willie Price's destiny will be: "Willie, abashed and guilty, found nothing to say. His eyes had the meek wistfulness of Holman Hunt's *Scapegoat*" (*AFT*, p. 222). Again, the adjective *meek* is a functional element in the definition of the character. Moreover, to make the young man's condition clearer, the narrator evokes a famous painting by William Holman Hunt (1827– 1910) precisely titled *The Scapegoat* (1854–56). In a sense, Willie becomes the sacrificial victim of a society that allows no room for errors. Hunt's painting, which was inspired by a verse from Leviticus, was defined by Madox Brown "one of the most tragic and impressive works in the annals of art". The quotation can be found on the website of the Manchester Art Gallery where the painting is kept: http://shop.manchestergalleries.org/scapegoat-holman-hunt-giclee-print-119-p.asp [last accessed 3 September, 2016]

78 Significantly, during the preparation for her wedding, Anna's thoughts are constantly of Willie Price, who becomes an obsessive presence in her mind: "[...] she never slept without thinking of Willie Price, and hoping that no further disaster might overtake him" (*AFT*, pp. 229–230).

congregation of which Ephraim is an elderly exponent is completely immersed in the logic of commercial calculation and the obsessive pursuit of wealth. Anna will therefore marry Mynors who embodies the entrepreneurial spirit of which the Methodism of the local community offers a moral justification for its materialistic ideology and ruthless struggle for survival. Anna's story is not simply the staging of the condition of a woman forced into silence and subordination, but also the story of a faith which is intertwined with the spirit of capitalism. The Methodism of the Five Towns has drifted so far apart from the preaching of John Wesley that is seems to have lost all idea of Christian forgiveness or humanist principles.

CHAPTER 3 Time and place in *The Old Wives' Tale*

1. *The Old Wives' Tale* is generally acknowledged to be Bennett's most important work[79]. Published in 1908, the novel marks a crucial moment in the writer's career interweaving the characteristic elements of his imaginative vision with his conception of human destiny. Like *Anna of the Five Towns*, *The Old Wives' Tale* is autobiographical in origin and draws its inspiration from the Potteries of the 1860s, the decade in which Bennett was born[80]. What particularly distinguishes it from Bennett's other works is the fact that the action is represented from within the apparent monotony of daily life. Before introducing the plot, however, it would be worthwhile considering the author's preface for the novel in which he reveals that the source of his inspiration was a ridiculous looking old woman he chanced to see in a restaurant in Paris in 1903[81]. After describing her in detail, he concludes: "Her case is a tragedy" ("Preface", *OWT*, p. 3).

---

79 See Walter Allen, *op. cit.*, pp. 321–323. Among the most convinced admirers of *The Old Wives' Tale*, Allen observes: "The Novel is the history of a community as well as of two old women [...] However much Bennett might try to emulate Maupassant, *The Old Wives' Tale* has a quite un-Naturalistic warmth. It is much less objective than it seems at first glance. [...] For what in the end characterizes *The Old Wives' Tale* is richness in order. Reading, one is aware all the time of the brilliance of character-creation and of invention; a whole world and epoch are brought to life. Yet everything has been sternly subordinated to Bennett's overriding conception, and one is left with the feeling that *never has the rhythm of ordinary life, life in time, been so faithfully, so surely transcribed*" (pp. 321–322, (my italics)

80 Hillis Miller, in the perceptive essay *On Literature*, in the chapter titled "Literature as Disguised Autobiography" highlights the author's role as the recorder of an experience that is subject to being narrated: "The writer is like a scientist or ethnographer writing a description of what he or she has found in a voyage of exploration". J. Hillis Miller, *op. cit.*, p. 104. In effect, Miller is saying that every author, even the most imaginative, cannot avoid drawing from their own experiences in the creative process.

81 As Bennett writes in the first page of the "Preface": "She was fat, shapeless, ugly, and grotesque. She had a ridiculous voice, and ridiculous gestures. It was

This episode seems to have led Bennett into imagining the kind of life the old woman could have led and, wondering about her past, he began to realise that she had once probably been charming and beautiful. His conclusion, therefore, can be summed up in the word; "tragedy", by which Bennett means the tragedy of time and the impossibility of confronting one's own past precisely because the individual lives its life directly. The supremacy of time lies in the impossibility of rectifying even one tiny instant of one's life as it moves on relentlessly, consuming everything.

Bennett also uses his preface to comment on the sense of human advancement within this uninterrupted flow of life. Taking femininity as a paradigm of beauty and its inevitable decline, the writer adds:

> [E]very stout ageing woman was once a young girl with the unique charm of youth in her form and movement and in her mind. And the fact that *the change from the young girl to the stout ageing woman is made up of an infinite number of infinitesimal changes, each unperceived by her, only intensifies the pathos* (*OWT*, pp. 3–4, my italics).

The other term which evidences Bennett's conception of the world is "change": The physical and mental transformations in the continuum of daily life are imperceptible to the individual because, as they travel through time – and grow old in time – they feel no revolutions or revelations in their transformation. Indeed, the deception lies in the very fact that time passes gradually. In this case, Bennett informs the reader that the extravagant woman he saw in the restaurant probably became stout and ugly without even realising it. The real tragedy of humanity is that people arrive at the end of their lives – and the awareness of their decrepitude – with no warning signs of their physical and mental changes.

In fact, as several critics have noted, behind Bennett's *Weltanschauung* lies the presence of Herbert Spencer who represents a line of thought culminating in social Darwinism. Thus, life is seen as an evolution in which those who know best how to adapt to the context have more of a chance to survive and thrive. It comes as no surprise therefore that Bennett considered Spencer's *First Principles* (1862), his point of reference and the fundamental text which, from a philosophical point of view, inspired all his works: "When I think how *First*

Principles, by filling me up with the sense of causation everywhere, has altered my whole view of life, and undoubtedly immensely improved it, I am confirmed in my opinion of that book. You can see *First Principles* in nearly every line I write"[82]. Bennett made this annotation in one of his *Journals* in October 1910 shortly after he had published *The Old Wives' Tale* and had confirmed for himself the image of time as a force which devours all things.

However, even more important here is the philosophical term "causation" which refers to a logical and temporal structure based on the relationship between cause and effect. Behind every individual choice there is always a cause that is more or less socially determined. For example, if one of the protagonists of the novel successfully manages a hotel in Paris, it is because she has been accustomed to living according to the economic and managerial logic of her family from a very early age. The extent to which Spencer's vision determines the destinies of the protagonists will be examined further on in a detailed analysis of the characters.

On a social level, *The Old Wives' Tale* reveals the changes in the behavioural and ethical and cultural codes of English society from 1863 to 1907 (effectively, from Bennett's birth till the publication of the novel). It may also justly be observed, with regard to the historical context of the novel, that Bennett may have been thinking of Dickens's *A Tale of Two Cities* (1859) – since the action in his novel takes place between the Five Towns of the Potteries and Paris, the two poles around which the destinies of Constance and Sophie Baines unravel.

The parallel transformation of society, observed in terms of the provincial and narrow-minded environment of the Potteries and the metropolitan world of Paris, also assumes a particular importance in the physical and psychological metamorphosis of the

---

easy to see that she lived alone, and that in the long lapse of years she had developed the kind of peculiarity which induces guffaws among the thoughtless", Arnold Bennett, *The Old Wives' Tale*, Oxford, Oxford University Press, 1995, p. 3. From now on all quotations are from this edition as *OWT* followed by page numbers.

82   Bennett, *The Journals*, cit., p. 335.

protagonists. Indeed, the action of the novel revolves around the opposition, on a social level, between the centre (Paris) and the periphery (the Five Towns). This contrast has a particular importance with regard to the lives of the two sisters in terms of their individual choices and socioeconomic development. As a result, the intricate interweaving of the lives of Constance and Sophia within the wider context of European society conveys an idea of temporality that recalls Spencer's principle of evolution as a matter of adaptation and adjustment. From this angle, the story of the Baines sisters may be read as a novel of formation in that, as they grow old, Constance and Sophia learn the tragic meaning of life as they each acquire their own different psychological and cultural identity. As Patricia Drechsel Tobin has noted, "The paradigmatic novel that is performed through time and pre-formed by Time is the *Bildungsroman*, the novel of a life-as-education wherein the *process* of a young life is projected as the *shape* that will govern its remaining years"[83]. It is in this sense that the text has the structure of a coming-of-age novel since – above all in the first part – the young lives of the protagonists reveal a series of attitudes which, on the socioeconomic and psychological level, have a decisive impact on them from the years of their maturity to their final days.

2. Before analyzing the narrative structure of *The Old Wives' Tale*, it would be useful to give an outline of the debate that Bennett provoked in Europe on the moment of its publication in October 1908. Before the novel was published, Bennett was generally held to be a fine, prolific narrator with an abundance of ideas and prolific. However, very few reviewers recognised his value and inventiveness. Now, a writer like H.G. Wells, after reading the novel, declared that he could at last respect Bennett twice more than in the past. However, it was not until 1920 that André Gide recognised *The Old Wives' Tale* as a masterpiece and urged for it to be translated into French. Gide wrote to Bennett in the following terms:

---

83   Patricia Drechsel Tobin, *Time and the Novel: The Genealogical Imperative*, Princeton, NJ, Princeton University Press, 1978, p. 5 (italics in the text).

Je sentais depuis longtemps qu'il me manquait de le connaître, et que je ne pourrais *bien* causer avec vous qu'ensuite. Mais à présent, ah! vous êtes ce que Flaubert eût appelé "un fameux gaillard"[84].

Thus, the critical fortune of the novel owes much to Gide who was one of the world's major literary figures at that time. The real problem behind the contemporary reviews in England was that the term 'realism' was often confused with 'naturalism'. Nevertheless, Bennett had no intention of writing a work which imitated or sought to compete with the realist tradition. His was a predominantly moralistic approach which presented the novel in terms of the truth rather than artistic experimentation:

> For some, the chief value of the novel lay in its scrupulous recording of innumerable truths about life, undistorted by any theory as to their composite meaning. Others, regarding realism as the inverse of romanticism, praised the book for its refusal to abandon the typical and its willingness to encompass the banal and the unpleasant[85].

Some studies did not fail to note that the novel succeeded in making the daily life of mundane things, devoid of sensationalism and revolution, interesting. Edward Garnett[86], who had been very critical of Bennett in a recent review, *The Grim Smile of the Five Towns*, immediately recognised the merits of *The Old Wives' Tale*: "Most novelists are rarely quite at one with their subject; a little above or below it, they enrich, romanticise, or impoverish it. But Mr Bennett really is his subject, the breath of it, intellectually, in a remarkable way"[87]. These words of appreciation by an influential literary figure like Garnett were

---

84 Linette F. Brugmans, (Introduction et Notes par), *Correspondance André Gide-Arnold Bennett: Vingt ans d'Amitié Litteraire (1911–1931)*, Genève, Librairie Droz, 1964, pp. 104–105 (italics in the text).

85 Squillace, *op. cit.*, p. 37.

86 Edward Garnett (1868–1937), writer and literary critic. Garnett was one of the most influential personalities of English culture during this period. As editor, he proposed the publication of D.H. Lawrence's *Sons and Lovers*. As editor of the major publishing houses of the time – T. Fisher Unwin, Gerald Duckworth e Jonathan Cape – he supported a series of more traditional writers such as John Galsworthy. As a literary critic, Garnett also gave an important contribution in promoting Russian literature (Tolstoy, Turgenev, etc.).

87 Edward Garnett's review appeared in *The Nation* on 21 November 1908, pp. 314 e 316.

enthusiastically received by Bennett who, on the strength of his new novel, was gaining consensus among intellectuals and men of culture. It was no accident that already in April 1909 Ford Madox Ford[88] asked him to collaborate for the new periodical *The English Review* – an invitation Bennett gladly accepted by offering the short-story "The Matador of the Five Towns".

In the following decades, the critical fortune of *The Old Wives' Tale* was reinforced with important contributions by John Wain and Margaret Drabble whose studies were committed to a re-evaluation of the novel in spite of the fact that it had been from the beginning an object of criticism on the part of those who were open supporters of modernism. In 1974, in her biography on Bennett,[89] Drabble, firmly convinced of Bennett's greatness, explored the writer's literary personality giving particular attention to his origins. As a result, she became a staunch defender of the author in spite of F.R. Leavis's[90] dismissal of Bennett as a second-class writer with no great qualities:

> My first reason for wanting to write this book was that I very much admired Arnold Bennett as a writer. I can't remember when I first read his novels but I liked them from the beginning. I started with the usual ones – *The Old Wives' Tale*, *Clayhanger* – and then moved on to his lesser known, and finally to his most frivolous books. And somewhat to my surprise, I liked them all. I'd been brought up to believe that even his best books weren't very good – Leavis dismisses him in a sentence or two, and not many people seemed to take him as seriously as I did. The best books I think are very fine indeed, on the highest level, deeply moving, original, and dealing with material that I had never before encountered in fiction, but only in life: I feel they have been underrated, and my

---

88   Ford Madox Ford was a friend of Edward Garnett. It is likely that Bennett's name as a collaborator for *The English Review* had been suggested to him by Garnett himself.

89   Drabble, *op. cit.*

90   See Leavis, *op. cit.* In particular the critic observes with a subtle irony: "[F]or all the generous sense of common humanity to be found in his best work, Bennett seems to me never to have been disturbed enough by life to come anywhere near greatness" (p. 16). Leavis's great tradition included Austen, Dickens, Henry James, Joseph Conrad and D. H. Lawrence. In reality, both Dickens and Lawrence were included in Leavis's great tradition in the second phase of his examination of the novel.

response to them is so constant, even after years of work on them, and constant rereadings, that I want to communicate my enthusiasm[91].

Drabble's reassessment of Bennett's work came at a time when writers were appreciated mainly for their social commitment as well as, for other reasons, their experimentalism. Bennett appeared to possess neither. Yet the biographer does not mince words in expressing her total admiration for an author she considers part of the great tradition of the English novel. It is also significant that in her biography she not only evidences the important inspiration of the Potteries but portrays Bennett in all his complexity, especially emphasising his European culture.

Still, in the early 1980s critics still maintained a rather simplistic notion of the author. Thus, Michael Bell, who edited a collected volume on the English novel of the first decades of the twentieth century, could only interpret Bennett's works through the same critical perspective which had been a commonplace at the beginning of his career. Tracing a parallel between Galsworthy and Bennett, Bell observes:

> John Galsworthy and Arnold Bennett continued to write the nineteenth-century realist novel: Bennett being the more substantial. Where Galsworthy's *The For-sythe Saga* becomes as flat as it is panoramic, Bennett in novels like *Anna of the Five Towns* (1902) or *The Old Wives' Tale* (1908) achieves a more satisfying solidity. It was, indeed, his relative success in this respect that led Woolf and Lawrence to single him out as the principal whipping boy when attempting to define their own aspirations[92].

Bennett would continually find himself compared to Galsworthy by his critics. According to Bell, it was precisely the ease with which he won the sympathy of his readers which attracted the criticism of Virginia Woolf and D. H. Lawrence. The latter, in particular, reproached him for his "emotional fatalism and the narrowness of his moral horizon"[93]. Lawrence also noted the influence of Zola who, similarly to Hardy and Gissing, had exerted a powerful effect on Bennett's works.

---

91   Drabble, *op. cit.*, p. ix.
92   Michael Bell, "Introduction: Modern Movements in Literature", in *The Context of English Literature 1900–1930*, ed. Michael Bell, London, Methuen, 1980, p. 80.
93   *Ibid.*

In a similar manner, John Wain referring to *The Old Wives' Tales*, underlined the fact that Bennett was the only English novelist who could successfully compete with the nineteenth century French tradition:

> It is one of the most successful attempts, if not *the* most successful, to rival in English the achievement of the French realistic novel from Balzac down through Flaubert, Zola and Maupassant[94].

It must be said that however much Bennett followed the model of the French novel, he created a language of his own in which nineteenth-century English fiction obviously played an important part, in spite of the fact that he considered it to be still too heavily dependent on moralistic discourse. Wain's interpretation is nevertheless limited to an emphasis of the historical importance of the novel to the detriment of its artistic presentation: "To Bennett, as to the realists in general, the three [historian, sociologist and novelist] had one aim: to discover, by patience and insight, the truth about the human being as they knew him in their time; and to pass on that truth with the minimum of distortion"[95]. John Holloway also observes, rather simplistically, that in Bennett's works, "the humanity of his characters [...] tends to be submerged in analysis of how they are the creatures of their environment"[96]. The critic also reasserts that Zola is the literary figure who most inspired Bennett's artistic experimentation, thus giving a disproportionate importance to the French writer whom, although admired by Bennett, only gave him the idea of an inseparable link between the environment and the psycho-social behaviour of character as is evident in *The Old Wives' Tale*:

> Bennett's sense of half-impersonal historical continuity (notably in *The Old Wives' Tale*, 1908), and his accumulation of factual detail to produce a dense and rich, if limited, context for the action, are achievements of no mean order; and the point, in the present context, is that such an achievement as they represent must certainly be related to the influence of Zola[97].

---

94   Wain, *op. cit.*, p. 7, (italics in the text).
95   Wain, "Arnold Bennett," in *Six Modern British Novelists*, ed. George Stade, New York, Columbia University Press, 1974, p. 9.
96   John Holloway, "The Literary Scene", *The New Pelican Guide to English Literature*, ed. Boris Ford, 8 vols., Harmondsworth, Penguin, 1986, *VII: From James to Eliot*, p. 71.
97   *Ibid.*

Although they recognise Bennett's value as a writer, both Wain and Holloway are guilty of a historical and sociological misunderstanding[98]. For them, the greatness of the novel resides in a conception of the world in which history and sociology converge in a determined way. However, while historical and sociological elements are always taken into account in novels, they have no importance on their artistic dimension in that they do not have the capacity to render a narrative text enjoyable for the reader. It is superfluous to add here that the great imaginative impact of *The Old Wives' Tale* concerns its unity of inspiration. It must be remembered that the adoption of the stylistic features of realism for Bennett was the best – if not the only – way to fully dramatize the transformations of two human lives within the complex web of social change and individual metamorphosis. It is certainly not only the precision of sociological details that gives a novel its power or its sole basis of truth, but the huge canvass of a world which experiences time and its erosion in terms of a subjectivity placed in a specific historical context. What interests Bennett, is this slow contraction which the two protagonists, after a phase of expansion (infancy, childhood, matrimony and children), undergo in a sort of return to a topological degree-zero. After being separated for decades, Constance and Sophia meet again and realise that everything has changed and that the real master of the world is the inexorable passing of time, while they are left to face the drama of old age, sickness and death.

3. The narrative expedients which govern the opening of a novel are much more complex than are initially apparent. As Edward W. Said observes: "Every writer knows that the choice of a beginning for what he will write is crucial not only because it determines much of what follows but also because a work's beginning is, practically speaking,

---

98   For Patrick Parrinder, beyond the influence of the nineteenth-century French masters, Bennett expresses a realism which finds its most convincing representation in his best works: "The Bennett of *Anna of the Five Towns* (1902), *The Old Wives' Tale* (1909), and *Clayhanger* (1910) remains unsurpassed as a realistic novelist of industrial and commercial England. Heroism in his novels is largely the heroism of self-restraint". Patrick Parrinder, *Nation and Novel: The English Novel from the Origins to the Present Day*, Oxford and New York, Oxford University Press, 2006, p. 288.

the main entrance to what it offers"[99]. The beginning is of fundamental importance precisely because it is the starting point for the development of the novel's themes and hermeneutic perspectives. Said also adds: "a beginning immediately establishes relationships with works already existing, relationships of either continuity or antagonism or some mixture of both"[100]. If we consider the opening lines of *The Old Wives' Tale*, two interconnecting discourse levels may be noted. On the one hand, it is easy to evidence the immediate reference (on an intratextual level) to a context – the Potteries – which represents a space of the memory and a source of images Bennett always uses in his works. On the other hand, on an intertextual level, the writer deliberately recalls the great novel tradition of the nineteenth-century (*Middlemarch* and the two sisters with which the novel opens immediately comes to mind[101]) and French Naturalism as defined by Zola and theorised in *Roman expérimental*. It is necessary therefore to proceed with an analysis of the opening of *The Old Wives' Tale* in the attempt to establish from the outset the themes of

---

99   Edward W. Said, *Beginnings: Intentions and Method*, New York, Columbia University Press, 1985, p. 3.

100 *Ibid.*

101 The reference to George Eliot's *Middlemarch* (1871–72) is no accident. In some respects, the initial images which indirectly compare the two sisters to two contrasting streams recall the epilogue of Eliot's novel in which the heroine adapts to her husband's needs by assuming a subordinate position: "Her finely-touched spirit had still its fine issues, though they were not widely visible. Her full nature, like that river of which Cyrus broke the strength, spent itself in channels which had no great name on the earth. But the effect of her being on those around her was incalculably diffusive: for the growing good of the world is partly dependent on unhistoric acts; and that things are not so ill with you and me as they might have been, is half owing to the number who lived faithfully a hidden life, and rest in unvisited tombs". (George Eliot, *Middlemarch*, ed. David Carroll, Oxford and New York, Oxford University Press, 1989, p. 682). See also Francesco Marroni, "Middlemarch e le metafore dell'eccesso", in *Middlemarch: il romanzo*, a cura di Anita Weston e John McRae, Napoli, Loffredo, 1987, pp. 11–31. In particular, Marroni writes: "The truth is that the image of the powerful stream which only if weakened can successfully spread its energy refers to a conception of narrative – as well as historical processes – as something that eludes any attempt at systematisation: novel and history both set up a text without a centre because both are products of an illusion" (p. 29, my translation).

the novel taking also into account the fact that, in his preface, Bennett reveals he has been inspired by Maupassant's *Une Vie*[102]:

> Here I must confess that, in 1908, I read *Une Vie* again, and in spite of a natural anxiety to differ from Mr. Bernard Shaw, I was gravely disappointed with it. It is a fine novel, but decidedly inferior to *Pierre et Jean* or even *Fort Comme la Mort*. To return to the year 1903. *Une Vie* relates the entire life history of a woman. I settled in the privacy of my own head that my book about the development of a young girl into a stout old lady must be the English *Une Vie*. I have been accused of every fault except a lack of self-confidence, and in a few weeks I settled a further point, namely that my book must "go one better" than *Une Vie*, and that to this end it must be the life-history of two women instead of only one. Hence, *The Old Wives' Tale* has two heroines. Constance was the original; Sophia was created out of bravado, just to indicate that I declined to consider Guy de Maupassant as the last forerunner of the deluge ("Preface", *OWT*, pp. 4–5).

Bennett characteristically establishes an ambivalent relationship with Maupassant marked by admiration and competition. Whilst he in no way denied the importance of the French writer, at the same time he declared that his reading of *Une Vie* in 1908 (during composition of *The Old Wives' Tale*), was a great disappointment compared with his enthusiastic reading of it in 1903. It seems obvious in this case that Bennett is attempting to belittle the imaginative impact of *Une Vie* so that the reader's approach to the novel is not intertextually conditioned.

Preliminary observations aside, we may now consider the first page of the novel in order to interpret its elements in terms of a hermeneutic reading[103]:

> Those two girls, Constance and Sophia Baines, paid no heed to the manifold interest of their situation, of which, indeed, they had never been conscious.

---

102 According to John Lucas, the fact that Bennett has Maupassant in mind during the writing of the novel is more a limitation than an advantage for *The Old Wives' Tale*. The influence of the French writer – and the competitive relationship with him – conditioned Bennett's inspiration. In this case, Lucas observes: "Its flaws do perhaps come from the French writer, or from something that was deep in Bennett himself and which attracted him to de Maupassant". John Lucas, *op. cit.*, p. 98.

103 Cfr. Michael Riffaterre, *Semiotics of Poetry*, Bloomington, IN, Bloomington University Press, 1984, pp. 4–5. Riffaterre also observes: "The second stage is that of retroactive reading. This is the time for a second interpretation, for the

They were, for example, established almost precisely on the fifty-third parallel of latitude. A little way to the north of them, in the creases of a hill famous for its religious orgies, rose the river Trent, the calm and characteristic stream of middle England. Somewhat further northwards, in the near neighbourhood of the highest public-house in the realm, rose two lesser rivers, the Dane and the Dove, which, quarrelling in early infancy, turned their back on each other, and, the one by favour of the Weaver and the other by favour of the Trent, watered between them the whole width of England and poured themselves respectively into the Irish Sea and the German Ocean. What a county of modest, unnoticed rivers! What a natural, simple county, content to fix its boundaries by these tortuous island brooks, with their comfortable names – Trent, Mease, Dove, Tern, Dane, Mees, Stour, Tame, and even hasty Severn! Not that the Severn is suitable to the county! In the county excess is deprecated. The county is happy in not exciting remark (*OWT*, p. 13).

After naming the main protagonists – the Baines sisters whose destinies are traced until the moment of their death – Bennett provides a series of contextual elements which are very important for establishing his central topological nucleus. The first spatial reference, which seems to follow the scientific dictates of a Naturalist approach, with its precise indication of the exact geographical latitude, seems entirely anticonventional. Also, the very title of the first chapter, "The Square", anticipates the descriptive nature of the first pages which, as will be seen, culminates in the representation of the Five Towns as a series of concentric circles. These increasingly widen until they narrow down again to focus on the family of the two sisters. "The Square" is not only a space where the novel begins, but the socioeconomic and psychological reality of the most important stories precisely because it is where the Baines family have their drapery shop. Consequently, this particular spatial entity presented in the incipit, besides being full of nuanced meanings[104], is diegetically the living centre of life not only in Bursley but the whole of the Potteries.

---

truly hermeneutic reading. As he progresses through the text, the reader remembers what he has just read and modifies his understanding of it in the light of what he is now decoding" (p. 5).

104 Bruno Traversetti e Stefano Andreani, *Incipit. Le tecniche dell'esordio nel romanzo europeo*, Torino, Nuova ERI, 1988, p. 17.

Immediately after the reference to the latitude, the attention is directed to the rivers of this particular area of England with the precise intention of indirectly communicating to the reader that there will be nothing exceptional about the lives of his protagonists. Indeed, the two little rivers mentioned – "the Dane and the Dove" – are described as insignificant and "quarrelling in early infancy" exactly like the two girls[105]. In this way, the writer suggests a parallel between the course of a river and the course of a life. The analogy is further emphasised by the fact that the two rivers separate with one pouring into the Irish Sea and the other ending its course in the German Ocean. In exactly the same way as the Dove and the Dane, the paths of the two sisters Constance and Sophia will also take opposite directions initially on a geographical level. In fact, while Constance remains tenaciously bound to the Potteries, Sophia decides to move to Paris where she remains for almost the whole of her life. However, this difference between them also relates to the psychological and behavioural level given that Constance embraces a traditional view of the world upon which she bases her whole life whilst Sophia bases the key moments of her life on transgression and romantic excess. The point to note here is the extent to which Bennett constructs his characters in terms of his naturalistic descriptions of space.

As if to reinforce the fact that his focus will be solely on the Baines sisters in the first chapter, the narrator assumes that they are the point of departure of his narrative. Moreover, from a purely diegetic angle their central importance is marked in terms of the oppositions convergence/divergence and affinity/diversity precisely in the same way in which the rivers Dove and Dane are represented:

> Constance and Sophia, busy with the intense preoccupations of youth, recked not of such matters. They were surrounded by the county. On every side the fields and moors of Staffordshire, intersected by roads and lanes, railways,

---

105 It has already been noted that the beginning of *The Old Wives' Tale* seems to be intertextually connected with the ending of *Middlemarch*. Another factor that cannot go unnoticed is that Bennett's novel describes two sisters just as *Middlemarch* begins with a description of the two sisters Dorothea and Celia Brooke, the one serious and committed to her role in society, the other frivolous and more concerned with realising her girlish romantic expectations.

watercourses and telegraph-lines, patterned by hedges, ornamented and made respectable by halls and genteel parks, enlivened by villages at the intersections, and warmly surveyed by the sun, spread out undulating. And trains were rushing round curves in deep cuttings, and carts and waggons trotting and jingling on the yellow roads, and long, narrow boats passing in a leisure majestic and infinite over the surface of the stolid canals; the rivers had only themselves to support, for Staffordshire rivers have remained virgin of keels to this day (*OWT*, p. 14).

The two sisters, who are almost the same age[106], have in common the thoughtlessness and light-heartedness of youth – time will soon reveal that this affinity will be the basis upon which their differences will emerge. At first, they seem destined to follow parallel lives, but their paths eventually diverge until they lose sight of each other. However, besides this preliminary consideration, as may be easily detected, Bennett adopts a cinematographic technique from the moment the focus is shifted from the protagonists to the countryside of Staffordshire where natural elements are interspersed with features of technology ("railways", "telegraph-lines", "trains", etc.) in the attempt to convey a complete image of the way nature communicates with the industrial world. It is no accident, therefore, that the second part of the passage quoted above mentions trains running on railway lines and boats sailing along canals in order to convey the sense of industriousness of labour and the work ethic which are such a dominant trait of this part of England.

As the focus widens to a long-range shot, the narrator describes the various activities performed in the countryside and the villages to narrow his focus again on the square and then from the square to the rooms in which the sisters live: "In short, the usual daily life of the county was proceeding with all its immense variety and importance; but though Constance and Sophia were in it they were not of it" (*OWT*, p. 14). The world beyond the drapery shop is wide and varied. Its multiple activities are not all connected with industry and commerce. Nevertheless,

---

106 In the second part of Chapter 1, the narrator offers a precise indication of their age difference which there is so small that they could almost be twins: "Their ages were sixteen and fifteen; it is an epoch when, if one is frank, one must admit that one has nothing to learn: one has learnt simply everything in the previous six months" (*OWT*, p. 18).

Constance and Sophia, who are locked in their tiny world and, no different to all the other adolescents in the county, live in a condition of
oblivion, naivety and infantile rivalry. Thus, in the first phase of their
lives the world and its problems are still very far away from Constance
and Sophia.

It is significant that Bennett does not take into consideration the
English landscape in general, but the Five Towns which he describes with
acute realism, particularly the world of commerce. With reference to the
district of the Potteries he highlights the unity in diversity of its individual towns:

> It lies on the face of the county like an insignificant stain, like a dark Pleiades in a
> green and empty sky. And Hanbridge has the shape of a horse and its rider, Bursley
> of half a donkey, Knype of a pair of trousers, Longshaw of an octopus, and little
> Turnhill of a beetle. The Five Towns seem to cling together for safety. Yet the idea
> of clinging together for safety would make them laugh. They are unique and indis-
> pensable. From the north of the county right down to the south they alone stand for
> civilization, applied science, organized manufacture, and the century – until you
> come to Wolverhampton. They are unique and indispensable because you cannot
> drink tea out of a teacup without the aid of the Five Towns; because you cannot eat
> a meal in decency without the aid of the Five Towns (*OWT*, p. 15).

Cinematically, the narrator's vision moves from inside the Baines
family home to the social and economic context in which the events
of the two sisters' lives occur. Here Bennett emphasises that the urban
reality of the Potteries is the result of different agglomerated villages –
Hanbridge, Bursley, Knype, Longshaw e Turnhill[107] – which make up a
fictional space based on a real space. From an imaginative viewpoint,

---

107 As far as the conglomeration of the Five Towns in concerned, it may be interesting to recall what Margaret Drabble writes: "Bennett created the Five Towns.
Once he had seen how to do it, he went ahead and made them. The reality of his
creation is at times confusing; many people think not of the Potteries as they
were, but of the Potteries as he described them. Even the names get mixed up.
There were in fact six towns, not five, but even serious newspaper articles have
to explain this, because for many readers Bennett's phrase, the Five Towns, has
stuck so firmly that it has more meaning than the places themselves. This is
partly the fault of his own method of providing pseudonyms: he stuck so close to
the original that he forgot which was which. Tunstall became Turnhill, Burslem
became Bursley, Hanley became Hanbridge, Stoke became Knype, Longton
became Longshaw, and Fenton he missed out altogether. On a similar scheme he

it appears as a stage crowded with characters who go through changes, contradictions and dilemmas. As Wellek and Warren observe: "Setting is environment; and environments, especially domestic interiors, may be viewed as metonymic, or metaphoric, expression of character. A man's house is an extension of himself". Describe it and you have described him[108]. In fact, in his awareness of the importance in establishing a functional link between description and narration, Bennett – like Hardy with his Wessex (where Dorchester becomes Casterbridge, Weymouth, Budmouth, Exeter, Exonbury etc) – recodifies the names of the towns so as to establish a space of the memory in which to bring his characters into life.

By giving an imaginary interpretation of the "insignificant stain" of the Five Towns, the writer highlights the difference between the natural and the urban landscape as he inscribes the urban outlines of the individual villages in a sequence of amusing figures: the horse and cavalier (Hanbridge), the little donkey (Bursley), a pair of trousers (Knype), an octopus (Longshaw) and finally a beetle for Turnhill. The effect is that of a puzzle which is pieced together into the precise topological entity of the Five Towns. Immediately after, the narrator again broadens the vision as if to proudly affirm the primacy of the Potteries and underline how in reality the "insignificant stain" on the map of the United Kingdom is itself a very important place for the purposes of glory and national commerce:

> *For this* the architecture of the Five Towns is an architecture of ovens and chimneys; *for this* its atmosphere is as black as its mud; *for this* it burns and smokes all night, so that Longshaw has been compared to hell; *for this* it is unlearned in the ways of agriculture, never having seen corn except as packing straw and in quartern loaves; *for this*, on the other hand, it comprehends the mysterious habits of fire and pure, sterile earth; *for this* it lives crammed together in slippery streets where the housewife must change white window-curtains at least once a fortnight if she wishes to remain respectable; *for this* it gets up in the mass at six a.m., winter and summer, and goes to bed when the public-houses close; *for this*

---

converts Waterloo Road into Trafalgar Road, Swan Bank into Duck Bank – this last a highly characteristic and appropriate touch of bathos". Drabble, *op. cit.*, pp. 3–4.

108 René Wellek and Austin Warren, *Theory of Literature*, Harmondsworth and New York, Penguin, 1978, p. 221.

it exists – that you may drink tea out of a teacup and toy with a chop on a plate. All the everyday crockery used in the kingdom is made in the Five Towns – all, and much besides (*OWT*, p. 15, my italics).

The anaphoric structure of this passage[109] highlights a kind of anxious desire on the part of the narrator to adequately account for the industrial patriotism that pervades the district whose factories are famous because they manufacture the ceramic products that can be found in every household in the United Kingdom and all around the world. The eight times repetition of the phrase *For this* indicates the urgency of finding an explanation for the existence of so many negative aspects of the Potteries (the mud, the pollution, the pervasive blackness and infernal smoke). But this ugliness is necessary for the production of beautiful objects which are not only the elegant cups and saucers with which the English drink their tea but also the precious objects which decorate the houses of the middle-class. Furthermore, this district which appears to bear the mark of negativity (precisely, a stain) has also produced great men and a wealth that contributes to the wellbeing of the nation:

A district capable of such gigantic manufacture, of such a perfect monopoly – and which finds energy also to produce coal and iron and great men – may be an insignificant stain on a county, considered geographically, but it is surely well justified in treating the county as its back garden once a week, and in blindly ignoring it the rest of the time (*OWT*, p. 15).

This almost triumphalistic description of the Five Towns is not an end in itself but functional to the representation of Bursley as a different place compared to the other towns of the Potteries – being the town and square in which the members of the Baines family live. In fact, in a sort of deterministic conception of the relationship between the individual and society, Bennett insists on defining all the details of the socioeconomic context, specifying the nuances that make one town different from another within the extended agglomeration. "the

---

109 Bennett's intention to construct the passage anaphorically, besides giving an idea of the circularity of the narrator's thoughts, evidences a certain patriotism which invites the narrator to take up a line of defence of the Potteries. From a rhetorical point of view, anaphora, as a figure of repetition, also gives a linguistic compactness and logical unity to the discourse on the level of meaning.

honours of antiquity in the Five Towns" (*OWT*, p. 16), it also has the great merit of being considered as the mother of all the towns in the Potteries. It is no accident, therefore, that the narrator is keen to specify the uniqueness of Bursley: "No industrial development can ever rob it of its superiority in age, which makes it absolutely sure in its conceit" (*OWT*, p. 16). Bursely is not only the centre of this specific geographical space, but it also has a square which, in this ancient town, is the centre of everyone's lives – "The Square was named after St Luke" (*OWT*, p. 16) –. Moreover, the windows of the Baines house look out onto the square in such a way as to almost represent its focal point. This is not only because the story concerns the Baines sisters but also because the large and famous family shop constitutes the culminating point of that space: "The aristocracy of the Square undoubtedly consisted of the drapers (for the bank was impersonal); and among the five the shop of Baines stood supreme" (*OWT*, p. 16).

In other words, the people who go to the square every day always have a very good reason to buy material from a family that is highly respected and wealthy in spite of the fact that for about twelve years the father, John Baines, has been confined to his bed and that the management of the flourishing activity has been passed on to his wife who guarantees that all the activity is conducted in the same disciplined, orderly and coherent way in which it was when John Baines himself was in charge. Mrs. Baines also inherits from her husband a certain traditional idea of how to manage trade which is very distant from the ostentatious self-advertising of modern trades. Indeed, Mr. Baines has always refused to replace the sign outside his shop that had been damaged by a violent gust of wind. Bursley always seems to be looking back to the past and the Baines faithfully interpret this attitude:

> For Constance and Sophia had the disadvantage of living in the middle-ages. The crinoline had not quite reached its full circumference, and the dress-improver had not even been thought of. In all the Five Towns there was not a public bath, nor a free library, nor a municipal park, nor a telephone, nor yet a board-school. People had not understood the vital necessity of going away to the seaside every year. Bishop Colenso had just staggered Christianity by his shameless notions on the Pentateuch. Half Lancashire was starving on account of the American war. Garroting was the chief amusement of the homicidal classes. Incredible as it may appear, there was nothing but a horse-tram running between Bursley and Hanbridge – and that only twice an hour; and between the other towns no stage

of any kind! One went to Longshaw as one now goes to Pekin. It was an era so
dark and backward that one might wonder how people could sleep in their beds
at night for thinking about their sad state (*OWT*, p. 23)[110].

This image of a society trapped in its own immobility contrasts with
the triumphalistic vision of the previous pages. Yet, the narrator does
not conceal his criticism of a community which appears incapable of
seeing beyond the geographical confines of the Five Towns. Obviously,
however, the facts are not quite as simple as this. Against the historical
stagnation that seems to characterise the Potteries, there is the mobility
of its products which not only reach the tiniest Hamlet of the nation,
but are sought for all over the world. In his ironic representation of the
social context, the reference to crinoline[111], besides giving the reader a
precise historical point of reference, shows an interpretation of reality
through feminine fashion, that is, through the point of view of a woman.

To be exact, the novel opens in 1862: the reference to the American Civil War (1861–1865) offers a very precise indication. In fact,
the interruption of supplies of raw cotton from the Southern Confe-
derate States deprived the manufacturing industries of Manchester
and caused an economic crisis. Bennett gives an accurate survey of
a variety of aspects of the 1860s, without neglecting to reference the
religious debate, above all because the geographical area in which the
story takes place was marked by a religious zeal connected to Methodism which had numerous converts in the Potteries It is in this context
that the phrase: "Bishop Colenso had just staggered Christianity by his
shameless notions on the Pentateuch" is inscribed. This is an explicit
reference to the Bishop of Natal, John William Colenso (1814–1883)
whose publication of *The Pentateuch and Book of Joshua Critically*

---

110 In the text "Pekin" as in the writer's manuscript. In the cited Penguin edition,
     with John Wain's introduction, this becomes "Peking" (p. 47), according to the
     commonly accepted GRAFIA. However, the original reads "Pekin" as in the
     Everyman's Library edition (London, Dent, 1966, p. 11).

111 It is well known that the French term *crinoline* means an open-weave fabric of
     horsehair or cotton that is usually stiffened and used specially for interlinings
     and millinery. In this narrative context it means a full stiff underskirt made of
     crinoline. This was introduced in 1863, although its adoption harks back to the
     fifties.

Examined (1863) had caused a heated religious controversy since it had questioned the historical accuracy and truth of the Old Testament.

A socio-cultural immobility seems to dominate the first pages of the novel with little sign of any future upheavals. However, despite the fact that Constance and Sophia live in "an era so dark and backward" and both seem isolated and without prospects like all the other inhabitants of the county, their stories will have a complex and varied development, with geographical dimensions stretching to Paris and destinies which are not simply the result of obscure and isolated lives. On the contrary, the socio-historical and political context which struggles to connect the towns of the Potteries even through the means of public transport, cannot help evidencing all the more the vivacity of the Baines sisters who in their ardent fantasies dream of a world different from their own. Thus, there emerges an opposition between the immobility of society and the anxious expectations of the sisters who are fully aware that reality does not end inside the walls of their father's shop.

4. *The Old Wives' Tale* is meticulously constructed with an equally precise symmetry. It is divided into four books, the first titled "Mrs. Baines", who is the main focus since she provides for everything given that her husband has been confined to bed for about twelve years. Book II ("Constance") and Book III ("Sophia") diegetically represent the most important part of the novel where the fates of the two sisters drift decisively apart. Finally, in Book IV ("What Life Is") the two sisters reunite after several decades and re-establish a link that lasts until their deaths – the first to die is Sophia while the novel concludes with the death of Constance. At this point, it must be observed that Bennett highlights the psychological and behavioural traits of the two sisters from the very first pages of the novel. Indeed, the first scene already clearly reveals how Constance's respect for rules is contrasted by Sophia's transgressive and, from the point of view of the nuclear family, destabilising view of life:

> Constance stayed her needle, and, without lifting her head, gazed, with eyes raised from the wool-work, motionless at the posturing figure of her sister. It was sacrilege that she was witnessing, a prodigious irreverence. She was conscious of an expectation that punishment would instantly fall on this daring impious child. But she, who never felt these mad, amazing impulses, could nevertheless only smile fearfully.

"Sophia!" she breathed, with an intensity of alarm that merged into condoning admiration. "Whatever will you do next?"

Sophia's lovely flushed face crowned the extraordinary structure like a blossom, scarcely controlling its laughter. She was as tall as her mother, and as imperious, as crested, and proud; and in spite of the pigtail, the girlish semi-circular comb, and the loose foal-like limbs, she could support as well as her mother the majesty of the gimp-embroidered dress. Her eyes sparkled with all the challenges of the untried virgin as she minced about the showroom. Abounding life inspired her movements. The confident and fierce joy of youth shone on her brow. "What thing on earth equals me?" she seemed to demand with enchanting and yet ruthless arrogance (*OWT*, pp. 24–25).

From a psychological-behavioural point of view, the first presentation of the two sisters already reveals certain traits which are confirmed by future events according to their respective fates. While Constance appears seriously concentrated and absorbed by her work, Sophia's mind is otherwise occupied. Her idea of wearing her mother's new dress without her parents knowing highlights at least three aspects of her character. The first concerns the enormous pleasure Sophia finds in her disobedience and, even more, putting into doubt the family order that has been imposed by her mother. In fact, Mrs. Baines acts as the real *pater familias* and sole manager of their property as well as exercising authority over the staff and her two daughters:

She was the daughter of a respected, bedridden draper in an insignificant town, lost in the central labyrinth of England, if you like; yet what manner of man, confronted with her, would or could have denied her naïve claim to dominion? She stood, in her mother's hoops, for the desire of the world. And in the innocence of her soul she knew it! The heart of a young girl mysteriously speaks and tells her of her power long ere she can use her power. If she can find nothing else to subdue, you may catch her in the early years subduing a gate-post or drawing homage from an empty chair. Sophia's experimental victim was Constance, with suspended needle and soft glance that shot out from the lowered face (*OWT*, p. 25).

In many ways, Sophia's daring action anticipates something that will be inscribed in the final phase of her life when, having lost all desire of breaking rules, she becomes the owner and excellent manager of a hotel in Paris. The narrator alludes to this deliberately: "The heart of a young girl mysteriously speaks and tells her of her power long ere she can use her power". However, what is important here is her disobedience which is inextricably linked with her exhibitionistic inclinations that is not without a capricious narcissism. Such distinctive signs of Sophia's character will form a centrifugal movement which will force her away from the Potteries and thus from a grey, enclosed and suffocating world.

At the opposite pole, the predominant direction of Constance's life is centripetal. Similar to the scene in which her sister wears their mother's dress, Constance becomes the victim of events and is forced to suffer rather than determine the development of the action – whether it concerns herself or others. The girl is therefore 'constant' in her obedience to the family codes and conventions and, in this respect, represents continuity. The first attitude in which she is presented is one of immobility where it is significant that she views her younger sister's behaviour as a form of 'sacrilege': "Constance stayed her needle, and, without lifting her head, gazed [...] motionless at the posturing figure of her sister". Not only does Constance consider the scene an act of sacrilege (that is, a profanation and deplorable lack of respect towards their mother) but also "a prodigious irreverence", convinced that she is witnessing an unimaginably foolish game. The contrast between Constance and Sophia could not be made more effective in this scene in which the psychological characteristics of the two sisters are defined once and for all. In a certain sense, it is already made evident that Constance represents the Five Towns, whilst Sophia represents the world that lies beyond the perimeters of the industrial complex.

Within this context is placed Mr. Povey who has a central role in the development of the narrative in terms of the continuity of the family. Although not yet twenty years-old, he is presented as an important figure because the drapery shop *is* Mr Povey – for the whole community, the Baines' commercial activity would be unimaginable without the presence of this dynamic, active young man who is absolutely faithful to the interests of commerce:

> He was Mr Povey, a person universally esteemed, both within and without the shop, the surrogate of bedridden Mr. Baines, the unfailing comfort and stand-by of Mrs. Baines, the fount and radiating centre of order and discipline in the shop; a quiet, diffident, secretive, tedious, and obstinate youngish man, absolutely faithful, absolutely efficient in his sphere; without brilliance, without distinction; perhaps rather little-minded, certainly narrow-minded; but what a force in the shop! The shop was inconceivable without Mr Povey. He was under twenty

and not out of his apprenticeship when Mr. Baines had been struck down, and he had at once proved his worth. Of the assistants, he alone slept in the house (*OWT*, p. 26).

In many respects, the adverb *universally* – which echos the opening of Austen's *Pride and Prejudice* – reflects a certain irony towards the efficient young apprentice who is already a surrogate of his boss and point of reference for Mrs Baines. Indeed, the introductory pages of the novel are all marked by proleptic/anticipatory elements as, in this case also, the image of Mr Povey already suggests his future marriage to Constance and role as the real manager of the family business. Thus, Mr Povey is a worthy young man who, because of his dedication to his work, cannot be confused with the other people who work in the shop.

It is also significant that Povey is a guest of the house – a sign of trust and consideration on the part of the Baines family which already says much about his role. Particularly revealing is the episode in which Povey complains to the concerned young girls of a terrible toothache. After giving him a double dose of laudanum ("four mortal dark drops", *OWT*, p. 31), Sophia, with her typical audacity, extracts a fragment of Povey's tooth while he is still asleep. For James Hepburn[112], the scene has clearly sexual connotations in that Sophia decides to keep for herself "a most perceptible, and even recognizable, fragment of Mr. Povey" (*OWT*, p. 33), whilst deceiving the young man that he has accidentally swallowed the piece of tooth. It is no accident, in fact, that the two young sisters quarrel for possession of the tooth in a sort of contest for ownership of a symbolic object. In the end it is the younger sister who has the upper hand:

> "It's only because I can't look at it without going off into fits!" Sophia gasped out. And she held up a tiny object in her left hand.
>
> Constance started, flushing. "You don't mean to say you've kept it!" she protested earnestly. "How horrid you are, Sophia! Give it me at once and let me throw it away. I never heard of such doings. Now give it me!"
>
> "No!", Sophia objected, still laughing. "I wouldn't part with it for worlds. It's too lovely" (*OWT*, p. 43).

---

112 James G. Hepburn, *The Art of Arnold Bennett*, Bloomington, IN, Indiana University Press, 1963, p. 28.

Again, the sisters' different behaviour towards others is made evident. For Constance, the fact that Sophia can make fun of the episode is scandalous. Indeed, there is an element of sexual deprivation in the way Sophia decides to keep the fragment of tooth for herself. For, to her, unlike Constance, Mr. Povey becomes a sexless figure. Squillace has justly observed that from a sexual point of view, the story of Sophia is that of a woman who "symbolically relieves men of their phalli several times"[113]. This apparently contrived Freudian interpretation come as no surprise. Bennett himself in a letter to his friend Elsie Herzog (dated 14 April 1912), suggests that his novel is full of signs and signals which may escape many, but are the result of an ingenious organisation of the plot: "Impossible for me to divine what are the mysterious passages in *The Old Wives' Tale* that puzzled you! I will however admit that no English novelist ever suggested more unspeakable things, and got away without being understood, than me in that book. I was inspired to make the attempt by Wells's assurance to me once that one could say what one liked even in an English novel, if one was ingenious enough"[114]. In a context in which Victorian culture was still predominant, "the unspeakable things" mentioned by Bennett could only be sexual references. In other words, the writer confirms that, in matters of sexuality, Sophia seems to be on the side of those who, initially fascinated by the idea of romantic adventure, conclude by viewing men with a profound sense of disdain as a result of their experiences. On the one hand, Constance's life follows the path of domesticity and a sexual continuity devoid of apparent visible shocks, on the other, Sophia's life follows a zig zag pattern characterised by discontinuity and unpredictability.

Sophia's attitude towards the fragment of Povey's tooth already reveals her perversity which, although never explicitly expressed, leads to a life of conflicts in love and scenes of violence, as when she witnesses a victim of the guillotine in Paris. Besides, the episode reveals not only the differences in the two sisters' personalities, but also a clear sense of conflict which, at the end of Chapter II ("The Tooth"), becomes palpable when Constance, in an excess of rage, secretly takes "the fragment of Mr. Povey, ran to the window, and frantically pushed the

---

113 Squillace, *op. cit*, p. 47.
114 Hepburn, *The Letters of Arnold Bennett*, cit., p. 310.

fragment through the slit into the Square" (pp. 44–45). For Sophia this is an act of transgression that is entirely uncharacteristic of her sister and, for this reason, all the more painful:

> She had accomplished this inconceivable transgression of the code of honour, beyond all undoing, before Sophia could recover from the stupefaction of seeing her sacred work-box impudently violated. In a single moment one of Sophia's chief ideals had been smashed utterly, and that by the sweetest, gentlest creature she had ever known. It was a revealing experience for Sophia – and also for Constance. [...] It was the moral aspect of the affair, and the astounding, inexplicable development in Constance's character, that staggered her into silent acceptance of the inevitable (*OWT*, p. 45).

As a result of their very different ways of interpreting, feeling and reacting to things, the sisters soon become suspicious of each other to the point that, although it may not be initially obvious, their paths gradually diverge until they no longer coincide at all.

The differences between the two women become more marked from the moment Constance confirms her intention to continue managing the shop and conducting all the activities connected to it. In her essential immobility she follows in the footsteps of her mother who makes no mystery of the fact that the furthest she has travelled in her life has been a journey to Manchester. This makes Mrs Baines an emblematic representative of the Potteries her daughter intends to emulate. Against Constance's conformism Sophia inhabits the dimension of transgression, declaring, to everyone's shock, that she wants to pursue her studies to become a teacher. From the point of view of the commercial middle-class such a choice seems a regression in comparison to the family's business. Teaching – and by extension any kind of cultural activity – have little to do with production or with the working activities of the commercial middle-class. This explains the mother's dismay when Sophia declares she will never work in the shop and has no intention of working for the family's clients. Significantly, she insists on continuing her studies so that, unlike Constance, she can work outside the square and beyond a world in which all the protagonists seem confined to act out their lives on a single stage.

From the psychological viewpoint of Mrs Baines, Sophia is a great disappointment in comparison with the positive acceptance of her parents on the part of her sister:

> Sophia was not a good child, and she obstinately denied in her heart the cardinal
> principle of family life, namely, that the parent has conferred on the offspring a
> supreme favour by bringing it into the world (*OWT*, p. 50).

The peculiar aspect of this quotation lies in its intense Victorian valence. Children had to show gratitude to their parents for being born and, as a consequence they were their parents' property in terms of their professional and sentimental choices. For this reason, the conflict with her mother becomes a clash between past and present, that is, the traditional woman clashes with the new need for independence on the part of the late Victorian generation. It is no accident that Constance and Sophia's teacher, Miss Aline Chetwynd, points out that "Sophia is by no means an ordinary girl" (*OWT*, p. 76). Although this phrase is apparently uttered without particular emphasis it is effectively a proleptic representation of the girl's future. For her life will really be extraordinary in terms of her psychological development and sentimental adventure not to mention the city she chooses to live in, Paris being the most evident antithesis to the narrow mindedness of the Potteries.

5. Bennett's symmetrical construction of the narrative of *The Old Wives' Tale* continues after Book I ("Mrs Baines") where the novel is divided into three other parts which correspond with the respective lives of the two protagonists (Book II "Constance" and Book III "Sophia") and Constance and Sophia's reunion after thirty years of separation (Book IV: "What Life Is"). It is notable that the writer describes the lives of the two heroines in the most detailed way possible without neglecting to highlight the Victorian context in which their existences unfold. Bennett's artistic approach proves worthy of such an impressive design precisely because he chooses to set every single episode in a world with which he is very familiar – whether it be the Five Towns or cities like London and Paris. Indeed, Bennett needs to dominate his narrative material in order to present everything through a realist perspective. This choice explains his decision to adopt an omniscient point of view, as with most nineteenth-century novels, without renouncing other descriptive possibilities such as free indirect discourse or limited point of view. For Squillace, this decision to represent diverse perspectives rather than a single central conscience reflects the writer's refusal to be a voice of authority:

Bennett's denial of authority to any single point of view, however objective, reflects a far broader rejection of authority. Indeed, *The Old Wives' Tale* is a definitely modern novel in that it continually identifies the modern with the anti-authoritarian. Rather than merely recording the recent past, Bennett simultaneously constructs and dismantles the Victorian era by encyclopaedically depicting it *as* past; he consigns to a Victorian England that he pretends to be dim and dead the innumerable paternalisms and repressions that he well knew endured into his own time. He particularly insists that the exposure of secrets is the death of Victorianism; the novel charts the progress of English character from self-isolation to self-advertisement, from the denial of desire to its cultivation[115].

In his representation of Victorian society, Bennett grasps all the signs of the transition towards a different lifestyle by focussing on the various levels of difficulty between the old and young generations to adapt. What was normal for Mrs Baines becomes an insult to her daughters' intelligence and offensive to their idea of self-accomplishment. For this reason, Bennett insists on the fact that Mrs Baines accepts Sophia's idea of continuing her studies as a grave violation of the behavioural codes of society. Indirectly, Bennett is suggesting that, for the Victorians, study and research were not considered proper activities for women for whom, other virtues competed which were more strictly connected with domestic life. If harmony and self-accomplishment means the complete refusal to change for Mr and Mrs Baines, it is quite the opposite for their daughters: Constance and Sophia view change as an opportunity for progress and, above all, the younger sister embraces unconditionally the idea that the traditional way of life and the society of the Potteries have no meaning in a world in which everything is continually transforming.

If this phenomenon is viewed from a Darwinian perspective the process of adaptation finds all the characters who cannot read the signs of the times forced to surrender, whilst the two sisters – albeit in their different ways – are able to interpret the new world and follow its flux. Yet the sisters are never presented as exceptional people. Indeed, even Sophia's act of transgression appears, in the context, a necessary choice given that control of the family business will be passed over

---

115 Squillace, *op. cit.*, pp. 43–44 (italics in the original).

to Constance. As Paul N. Siegel has noted: "These ordinary people, however, are presented in a finely visualized world which changes as they change. *The Old Wives' Tale* is concerned with the development of English middle-class society from 1863, when the novel begins, until 1907, when it ends, as well as with the development of its characters"[116]. It is fitting to conclude that from the point of view of its social transformations, *The Old Wives' Tale* may be considered a Darwinian novel. Thus, when the two sisters meet again and embrace each other after being apart for thirty years, they have not simply grown old, but also discover their differences – each having a different mentality and interpretation of things. In this respect, it is obvious that Constance, who lives secluded in her shop for thirty years is very different from Sophia who, in the same period has experienced directly political and social revolutions in Paris. Yet, for both, life has meant change and a simultaneous process of adaptation. If they are still alive and can meet each other it is because, unlike everyone else, they have succeeded in adapting and following the traumatic events of History and not found themselves on the side of the defeated who have succumbed to change.

In Book II the forms and strategies of adjustment with respect to the events that occur in Bursley suggest that the profound trauma of Sophia's escape with Gerald Scales, as a result of which the girl establishes a romance and dreams of worlds far away from the stifling environment of the provincial town, has been overcome. After their marriage, Scales turns out to be very different from the romantic and loyal person Sophia has imagined him to be. Nevertheless, in Chapter V of Book I ("The Traveller"), the young man appears to her as a means of salvation:

> *She was in a state of ecstatic, unreasonable, inexplicable happiness.* All her misery, doubts, despair, rancour, churlishness, had disappeared. She was as softly gentle as Constance. Her eyes were the eyes of a fawn, and her gestures delicious in their modest and sensitive grace. [...] *He excelled all her dreams of the ideal man.* His smile, his voice, his hand, his hair – never were such! Why, when he spoke – it was positively music! When he smiled – it was heaven! His smile, to Sophia, was one of those natural phenomena which are so lovely that they make

---

116 Paul N. Siegel, "Revolution and Evolution in Bennett's *The Old Wives' Tale*", *Clio*, 4, 2 (1975) p. 159.

you want to shed tears. There is no hyperbole in this description of Sophia's sensations, but rather an understatement of them. She was utterly obsessed by the unique qualities of Mr. Scales. Nothing would have persuaded her that the peer of Mr. Scales existed among men, or could possibly exist. And it was her intense and profound conviction of his complete pre-eminence that gave him, as he sat there in the rocking-chair in her mother's parlour, that air of the unreal and the incredible (*OWT*, p. 111, corsivi miei).

A characteristic trait of the young Sophia is her search for romantic adventures at all costs and the encounter with Gerald Scale seems to promise her the happiness she has been seeking. In her mind, Gerald, who comes from a different world to the unrefined Bursley, embodies only positive values. She sees him as the ideal man who will free her from the family prison[117]. This facile tendency to self-aggrandisement naturally weakens with the passing years and – as often occurs – leads her in the opposite direction to the point that she becomes cynical of men and loses all her illusions about love. As the narrator points out, there is nothing hyperbolic about the description of Sophia's sensations. On the contrary, they correspond to reality. In exactly the same way that all the goodness in the world is concentrated on Mr. Scale – after their marriage – all the evil of the world is concentrated on the same man. As Martha Nussbaum writes, "Literature focuses on the possible, inviting its readers to wonder about themselves"[118]. In this wide range of possibilities is inscribed the paradox embodied by Scales in his relationship with a heroine who sees him as an ideal hero who will free her from the monstrously puritanical society of the Potteries.

---

117 In Sophia's excited mind the real hyperbolic representation of Gerald Scales occurs a few pages later when the girl establishes a more explicit association between the lover and the idea of culture based on the image of Paris as the centre of the world. It is at this point that Gerald becomes her hero to whom she can entrust her body and soul: "She was deeply impressed. He was a much greater personage than she had guessed. It had never occurred to her that commercial travellers had to go to a university to finish their complex education. And then, Paris! Paris meant absolutely nothing to her but pure, impossible, unattainable romance. And he had been there! The clouds of glory were around him. He was a hero, dazzling. He had come to her out of another world. He was her miracle. He was almost too miraculous to be true" (*OWT*, p. 130).

118 Martha C. Nussbaum, *Poetic Justice: The Literary Imagination and Public Life*, Boston, Beacon Press, 2004, p. 5.

The uniqueness of Sophia's life contrasts with Constance's acceptance of normality, which, as has been evidenced, represents the continuity that never betrays the pulsating heart of the Potteries. From a visual angle, even the apparently antiromantic environment of the Five Towns has a certain aura of mystery, an element of excitement and adventure, even though less evident than London, Paris or other European capitals. It is always a question of point of view: "The romance in Arnold Bennett is the romance of the real. It is a thoughtful romance. And it is romance tinctured with irony. It is that vision of human experience whereby the everyday, the commonplace, the humdrum, is seen, stripped of the wrappage of familiarity"[119]. Thus, even Constance's life has its moments of enthusiasm and excitement in spite of the fact that the world around her seems to deny it.

Nevertheless, her decision to marry Samuel Povey can only be seen as a question of continuity in commercial terms as well as in terms of the family unity since the boy has always been considered an integral part of the household. Significantly, however, their wedding occurs offstage. The reader learns that Povey has declared himself to Constance who is reticent and does not take a decision since, unlike with Sophia, her mother is still in control of her destiny:

> From a practical point of view the match would be ideal: no fault could be found with it on that side. But Mrs Baines could not extinguish the idea that it would be a 'comedown' for her daughter. Who, after all, was Mr Povey? Mr Povey was nobody (*OWT*, p. 146).

Once again, Mrs Baines embodies tradition and, what is more important, the spirit of one who views matrimony as a means of social advancement. In this respect, Povey represents a regression for the Baines' family even though the woman is aware that in terms of the family interests (and thus of continuity) Samuel Povey would render the shop's position more stable precisely because he is also a man in whom she can trust and who knows every aspect of their commercial activity. In the epilogue to Book I we learn that Povey is now Constance's husband and that Mrs Baines has abandoned Bursley to live with her sister in

---

119 Sidney Hayes Cox, "Romance in Arnold Bennett", *The Sewanee Review*, 28, 3 (July 1920) p. 366.

defeat and disappointment after a life of projects and hopes she had nurtured for her daughters, her shop and the future of the Bains family:

> And Mrs. Baines said: "My life is over". It was, though she was scarcely fifty. She felt old, old and beaten. She had fought and been vanquished. The everlasting purpose had been too much for her. Virtue had gone out of her – the virtue to hold up her head and look the Square in the face. She, the wife of John Baines! She, a Syme of Axe!
>
> Old houses, in the course of their history, see sad sights, and never forget them! And ever since, in the solemn physiognomy of the triple house of John Baines at the corner of St. Luke's Square and King Street, have remained the traces of the sight it saw on the morning of the afternoon when Mr. and Mrs. Povey returned from their honeymoon – the sight of Mrs. Baines getting into the waggonette for Axe; Mrs. Baines, encumbered with trunks and parcels, leaving the scene of her struggles and her defeat, whither she had once come as slim as a wand, to return stout and heavy, and heavy-hearted, to her childhood; content to live with her grandiose sister until such time as she should be ready for burial! The grimy and impassive old house perhaps heard her heart saying: "Only yesterday they were little girls, ever so tiny, and now –" The driving-off of a waggonette can be a dreadful thing (*OWT*, p. 152).

The epilogue to Book I is not simply Mrs Baines declaration of surrender before a reality she can no longer understand. On a more universal and less subjective level, we may conclude that we are presented with a so-called heterogeny of ends: things have gone differently to the way in which Mrs Bains had imagined. A time comes when one realises that one's projects have only been realised in part or not at all. Compared to one's expectations, the outcome is a failure and, together with the sense of failure, like Mrs Bains, one is convinced that life no longer has any meaning. In the case of Bennett's character, although she is only fifty years-old, she feels the unbearable weight of time on her shoulders. Time has passed inexorably consuming everything. Mr Bains's long illness and his death, Sophia's rebellious temperament, and her marriage leave the woman with only "sad sights" that no positive event can ever redeem.

Everything is transformed while Mrs Baines, unable to adapt to change or to come to terms with a new world, is forced to succumb and leave the managing of the commercial activity to younger forces. In this transformation, space assumes a particular role. Mrs Baine's life is linked to the vision of St Luke's Square as an expression of the certainty of her being at the centre of provincial life – the square means crowds of people passing by and living their daily lives ignoring the fact that tragedy and conflict are always round the corner. Even more than the square, the house is a part of Mrs Baine's personality precisely because she has lived the most important moments of her life there[120] – yet, after many years, she decides to leave the house to return to the place of her origins at Axe. Although it is a different town where she lives in a different house, the presence of her sister Harriet makes her old age less bitter after she has painfully left behind her "the scene of her struggle and her defeat".

What emerges in the conclusion is a sense of time that is beyond Mrs Baine's control and which suddenly reveals to her that "only yesterday" Constance and Sophia were two lively girls who animated her house. If "yesterday" metaphorically represents many years previously, it is also a stretch of time that seems very near to her, as if the many years were consumed in a few hours – the opposition *yesterday/now* almost overlaps since between *now* and *yesterday* there seems to be the space for one breath: "Only yesterday they were little girls, ever so tiny, and now –" Time is therefore the protagonist of Mrs Baine's mental stage as she connects her defeat to the syntagm "only yesterday" which concludes her life in St Luke's Square. It also cannot go unnoticed that the final words of Book I refer to a few pages earlier in which Mrs. Baines anticipates her conscious acquisition of the deceitfulness of time and its consequent sadness[121]:

---

120 The fact that Mrs Baines makes the autonomous decision to leave her house in St Luke's Square does not diminish its traumatic impact. As Saunders writes, "Houses, for Bennett, were not a substitution for character; they were part of one's character and life. Inspired, to some extent, by naturalism, which regarded the material world as an inextricable influence on character and action, Bennett saw where one lived, how one lived and how one arranged one's material possessions to be expressive of personality, identity and self-development". Angharad Saunders, "Interpretation of an Interior", *Literary Geography*, 1, 2 (2015), p. 179.

121 John Lucas justly detects a paradigm of sadness and melancholy that appears evident at the conclusion of Book I: "[I]t cannot be denied that running through the novel there is streak of something which it is perhaps more accurate to call melancholy rather than misery, often submerged but sometimes rising to gleam blackly through its study of provincial lives". Lucas, *op. cit.*, p. 107.

Only yesterday, it seemed to Mrs. Baines, she had borne Sophia; *only yesterday* she was a baby, a schoolgirl to be smacked. *The years rolled up in a few hours*. And *now* she was sending telegrams from a place called Charing Cross! How unlike was the hand of the telegram to Sophia's hand! How mysteriously curt and inhuman was that official hand, as Mrs. Baines stared at it through red, wet eyes! (*OWT*, p. 151, corsivi miei).

In his conscious search for a thematic and aesthetic compactness, Bennett adopts the point of view of Mrs Baines in the final pages of Book I as the locus from which change and, above all, the irony implicit in change is perceived. Just as she is about to abandon Bursley, the woman is struck by the painful awareness of her fragility which is also the fragility of every human being. The reiterated evocation of the image of Constance and Sophia when they were only two little girls conceals a more general lesson that concerns the human condition and the ironic valence that underlies it. Whilst happy parents observe their children who grow day by day, learn their first words and begin to become autonomous, they do not realise that time also passes for them – they do not realise that the price for the happiness they receive from their children is decline and old-age. Time makes concessions for no-one. It is with this awareness that Mrs Baines leaves the house to Samuel Povey and Constance who, as husband and wife[122], begin to inevitably repeat the

---

122 It must be noted here that at the end of Book I Mrs Baines cannot help realising that both of her daughters have disappointed her expectations. As mentioned above, Samuel Povey may be a good boy in her estimate but he is still only a shopkeeper. The loss of social status is also evidenced by the life of Povey's older brother Daniel, who marries a sloppy woman with dubious morals addicted to alcohol. After years of patience and tolerance, he kills her in a moment of rage. The episode, albeit indirectly, is a smear on Samuel's image as he selflessly attempts to help his brother. In light of Daniel and his dead wife, Samuel Povey also cannot help reflecting on the inexorable passing of time: "And by the door stood her husband, neat, spotless, almost stately, the man who for thirty years had marshalled all his immense pride to suffer this woman, the jolly man who had laughed through thick and thin! Samuel remembered when they were married. And he remembered when, years after their marriage, she was still as pretty, artificial, coquettish, and adamantine in her caprices as a young harlot with a fool at her feet. Time and the slow wrath of God had changed her" (*OWT*, pp. 237–238). Samuel fails to save his brother from the gallows but the narrative voice reiterates his goodness from the moment he himself dies of pneumonia

same story in which happiness and pain are inextricably linked in the inexorable flux of time.

6. A detailed description of the various diegetic networks that make up the complex web of a plot grounded on a double spatial polarity does not fall within the scope of this study. However, it seems obvious that the element of 'disorder' is represented by Sophia who, from the moment she is born, is destined to a life of transgression. Her rebelliousness implies a total distance from the Five Towns with her consequent choice of Paris as the metropolitan space which is the most representative of the spirit of transgression. It is no accident therefore that Book III is entirely dedicated to Sophia and that the first chapter is titled "The Elopement" in which her sentimental adventure culminates in the most transgressive gesture possible, at least from the point of view of Victorian orthodoxy: living with a man outside marriage. However, as the human imagination often creates what reality deconstructs, this new life immediately reveals itself to be less romantic than Sophia believed whilst Gerald Scales, in turn, reveals himself to be less trustworthy than he initially appears once their union is legalised.

Significantly, in the first chapter the heroine has a sorrowful anticipation of her life in Paris where her dreams will never be fulfilled and, realising the impossibility of ever being able to go back and change her mind, she allows herself to be defeated "as helpless as a rabbit in London" (*OWT*, p. 314). As she accumulates experience, Sophia manages to emerge from her condition of solitude and poverty years later. In the meantime, on July 1 1866 (as the narrator notes exactly), at the beginning of her adventure, she is compelled to cope with a world that suddenly appears foreign, aggressive and devoid of solidarity and sympathy:

> An enormous folly! Yes, an elopement; but not like a real elopement; always unreal! She had always known that it was only an imitation of an elopement, and must end in some awful disappointment. She had never truly wanted to run away; but something within her had pricked her forward in spite of her protests.

---

at the end of Chapter V as a consequence of attempting to defend Daniel: "He lacked individuality. He was little. I have often laughed at Samuel Povey. But I liked him and respected him. He was a very honest man [...] He embraced a cause, lost it, and died of it" (*OWT*, p. 264).

> The strict notions of her elderly relatives were right after all. It was she who had been wrong. And it was she who would have to pay.
>
> "I've been a wicked girl", she said to herself grimly, in the midst of her ruin (*OWT*, p. 313).

From the point of view of her psychological development[123], through the technique of the internal monologue, Bennett highlights the consciousness of the nineteen-year-old heroine who, faced with the postponement of her wedding in London (before her departure for France), begins to suspect that "he was using the classic device of the seducer" (*OWT*, p. 309). Thus, the reader is given the first negative sign of the man who, once in Paris, reveals himself to be superficial and dishonest towards the girl. The fact that at the very first difficulty Sophia is plagued by doubts regarding her choice reveals the drama of her torn conscience in which such chaos reigns that she suddenly discovers that "her mind was a foreign country" (*OWT*, p. 309):

> She faced the fact. But she would not repent; at any rate she would never sit on that stool. She would not exchange the remains of her pride for the means of escape from the worst misery that life could offer. On that point she knew herself. And she set to work to repair and renew her pride.
>
> Whatever happened she would not return to the Five Towns. She could not, because she had stolen money from her Aunt Harriet (*OWT*, p. 313).

Still, at the end of the chapter, the young man solves the problem of their marriage and re-establishes his position of dominance with respect to the girl: "Gerald resumed his perfection again in her eyes! He was the soul of goodness and honour!" (*OWT*, p. 317). What is important to underline here is Sophia's pride. For rather than face the prospect of returning to the gloomy provincial world from which she has fled she is willing to face life alone. Although this does not immediately happen, loneliness will be her destiny. In the meanwhile, her existential

---

123   In the complex organization of the novel the great space reserved for the investigation of the inner universe of the protagonists produces, as Agosti suggests in his book on novelistic strategies, a crack at the concept of truth underlying the ideological frame of nineteenth-century novel. On this point see Stefano Agosti, *Enunciazione e racconto: per una semiologia della voce narrativa*, Bologna, il Mulino, 1989, pp. 11–13.

experience with Gerald is in many ways anticipated. For in spite of the fact that their union has been sanctioned by a wedding in London, his ardently erotic imagination continues to regard his wife as "the ideal mistress".

On a practical level, the story of Sophia in Paris is that of a spirit who, after reaching a culminating point in the first moment of her sojourn as a married woman, gradually goes through a decline until she sinks into the darkest pessimism. The first phase of her biography concerns this fall and loss of faith in the whole of humanity whilst the second phase sees her determination to re-emerge adopting every possible weapon without any kind of scruple and armed with cynicism and cold calculation. However, the narrator punctually registers the moment of loneliness and depression on the part of Sophia in the fourth section of Chapter IV ("A Crisis for Gerald"):

> She passed a night of physical misery, exasperated by the tireless rattling vitality of the street. She kept saying to herself: "I'm all alone now, and I'm going to be ill. I am ill". She saw herself dying in Paris, and heard the expressions of facile sympathy and idle curiosity drawn forth by the sight of the dead body of this foreign woman in a little Paris hotel (*OWT*, p. 368).

Unlike Constance, whose destiny – albeit varied and complex – is devoid of great upheavals,[124], Sophia's life is characterised by a series of crisis – arguments with the family, with her sister and her husband and society in general. Besides signalling the decisive moments of her

---

124 In the economy of the novel, Constance's son, Cyril Povey, is a destabilising element in the continuity of her family life. Unlike his father Samuel and his mother, he decides he does not want to work for the family business. Cyril represents an element of non-disjunction between his mother and his aunt Sophia from the moment he decides to abandon the Potteries just like his aunt – and live in Chelsea where he studies to become a sculptor. Here he comes into contact with artists and friends among whom Matthew Peel-Swynnerton. The latter will meet Sophia in Paris. These events occur when Cyril is about twenty years-old and is heedless of his mother's destiny. Book IV significantly begins with Peel-Swynnerton's discovery of the woman's role as a landlady: "If this Mrs Scales was the long-vanished aunt of his friend, Cyril Povey, she must know those two names, locally so famous. Did she start? Did she show a sign of being perturbed?" (*OWT*, p. 469).

life as a rebellious woman, these crises are the consequence of her irrational enthusiasms which initially raise her spirits to great heights only to send her crashing painfully down. Ultimately, she is one of the most successful creations of Bennett's fervid imagination. For through Sophia's torments and psychological instability, the writer dramatizes the restless years of an era in transition in which English society seems to be searching for itself both in terms of an overcoming of Victorian values and of a resistance to change. John Lucas does not exaggerate when he affirms that:

> The whole of Book 3 is a triumph of Bennett's art. Whether he is writing about Sophia's elopement with Gerald Scales, his desertion of her in Paris, her struggle to survive, her eventual triumph as owner of Frensham's, the small Paris pension, or whether he is writing about her tangles with other women and her rejection of proffered love, Bennett writes and imagines flawlessly[125].

In fact, Sophia is also Bennett's most successful character because her condition of exile is deeply authentic. Bennett is describing his own struggle to proudly survive the little daily misfortunes by always observing his protagonist from both an external and internal viewpoint. This double perspective is what makes the heroine so credible because her reflections are the logical consequence of the context, that is of the external reality of her daily life without illusions or enthusiasms:

> Her reputation for sagacity, for commonsense, was, she knew, enormous; she always felt, when people were talking to her, that they regarded her as a very unusually wise woman. And yet she had been guilty of the capital folly of cutting herself off from her family. She was ageing, and she was alone in the world. She was enriching herself; she had the most perfectly managed and the most respectable Pension in the world (she sincerely believed), and she was alone in the world (*OWT*, p. 481).

This quotation shows Bennett's ability to represent the respective existences of the Baines sisters in terms of their psychological transformation in comparison with their fundamentally immobile character traits. Through free indirect discourse the narrator reveals how, in the age of reason ("a very unusually wise woman"), Sophia has acquired a sagacity

---

125 Lucas, *op. cit.*, p. 109.

that she did not possess when, as a sixteen-year-old she rebelled against her family and fled with her lover. From the perspective of her maturity, she now views her past behaviour as "the capital folly". A series of erroneous decisions force her to conclude that the euphoric world of her childhood was an error for which she is now forced to pay with a loneliness that carries the bitter taste of being far away from the people who have loved her and watched her grow into an independent woman. From this angle, both of her parents as well as her older sister acquire a moral importance that Sophia was not able or did not want to understand. Now, she is faced with an extreme loneliness for which she has no remedy – a loneliness that seems all the more painful because the idea takes root in her that, sooner or later, she is bound to die:

> She was the most solitary person on earth. She had heard no word of Gerald, no word of anybody. Nobody whatever could truly be interested in her fate. This was what she had achieved after a quarter of a century of ceaseless labour and anxiety, during which she had not once been away from the Rue Lord Byron for more than thirty hours at a stretch. It was appalling – the passage of years; and the passage of years would grow more appalling. Ten years hence, where would she be? She pictured herself dying. Horrible! (*OWT*, p. 481).

For Sophia the time has come to assess her life. After twenty-five years of struggle to survive and affirm her dignity as a woman, her future appears bleak and hopeless: the harvest of "a quarter of a century" means only fatigue and anxiety. And the result of her defeat that implies, in the end, the return to her origins in Bursley from where she had fled because she was horrified by that narrow-minded world. Now, in her maturity what horrifies her is Paris whose axiological horizon she no longer recognises and that has become a city devoid of values, and positive memories.

Before surrendering to the idea of returning to the world of the Potteries, Sophia opposes a determined resistance because in spite of her existential failure, she is still proud of being a rebel to the conformism of her family: "She was without a plan. Her brain told her that she ought to return to Bursley, or, at the least, write. But pride would not hear of such a surrender. [...] She would face any disaster, and any other shame, rather than the shame of her family's forgiving reception of her" (*OWT*, p. 401). Therefore, her return home after so long is seen by Sophia as a form of surrender and disgrace. Better a life of hardship than an act of humility before the family and the society of the Five Towns. Yet, in the end she is forced to surrender. Her proud resistance is broken down by a letter from her sister in reply to an initial contact established through Matthew Peel-Swynnerton, a friend of Constance's son, who, by a series of coincidences, functions as a go-between for the two sisters separated by distance and time:

> Cyril is the name of my son. I married Samuel in 1867. Cyril was born in 1874 at Christmas. He is now twenty-two, and doing very well in London as a student of sculpture, though so young. He won a National Scholarship. There were only eight, of which he won one, in all England. Samuel died in 1888. If you read the papers you must have seen about the Povey affair. I mean of course Mr. Daniel Povey, Confectioner. It was that that killed poor Samuel. Poor mother died in 1875. It doesn't seem so long. Aunt Harriet and Aunt Maria are both dead. Old Dr. Harrop is dead, and his son has practically retired. He has a partner, a Scotchman. Mr. Critchlow has married Miss Insull. Did you ever hear of such a thing? They have taken over the shop, and I live in the house part, the other being bricked up. Business in the Square is not what it used to be. The steam trams take all the custom to Hanbridge, and they are talking of electric trams, but I dare say it is only talk. I have a fairly good servant. She has been with me a long time, but servants are not what they were. I keep pretty well, except for my sciatica and palpitation. Since Cyril went to London *I have been very lonely* (*OWT*, p. 486, my italics).

The long letter Constance writes to her sister appears, at least on the surface, as a report of facts that have occurred in the meantime, with the first mention of the birth of her only child. Following this is a series of events in which death seems to be predominant, beginning with that of her husband Samuel which is an indirect consequence of the fate of his brother Daniel who is sentenced to death for having murdered his wife. The deaths of Mrs Baines and the two aunts Harriett and Maria complete a letter full of bitterness and gloom. Behind the succession of dates and events lies the paradigm of temporality as the dominant element of the whole message.

It is not, as Lodge suggests, a question of underlining the fact that Bennett is conveying to his readers "an unproblematic rendering of social reality"[126], but rather that his discourse is always connected on

---

126 David Lodge, *Consciousness and the Novel*, London, Penguin, 2002, p. 119.

the level of the individual conscience so that social problems are filte-
red through the eyes of the protagonist. This is why the narrator is not
so much interested in showing the events of history as such but how the
facts of history are interpreted by individuals – such as Sophia in Paris
during the Franco-Prussian War which culminated with the defeat of
Napoleon III in Sedan on 1° October 1870. The reader only comes to
know of historical events through the heroine's conscience.[127].

However, at the centre of the narrative discourse there always
remains the flux of time which implies the transient presence of human
beings in the world. Deep down, Bennett is aiming to convey precisely
this sense of transience to his readers: the precariousness of human life
that time punishes with old age which, as Bennett himself declares in
his "Preface" is an absolute condemnation. In this condition, human
beings – like the old woman in the restaurant in Rue de Clichy – become
ridiculous and pathetic. And such "ridiculous mannerisms" (Preface,
OWT, p. 3) embody the visible expression of an external decadence that
conceals a pervasive internal corruption. Thus, the world of Bennett's
artistic vision points precisely to this ruthless portrait of the individual. In this framework is enclosed the condition of loneliness to which
Constance refers with the painful awareness that she cannot count on
her son Cyril. At this point of the narration loneliness is what unites the
sisters whose destinies after years of separation seem to converge on
this realisation – that they are two lonely women who, just as when they
were little girls, now have the possibility to keep each other company
again. Everything seems to come full circle for the two sisters: what
has been is again present in their lives. Yet, at the same time, this is not
the way things really are. For when they were girls, they both looked
with expectation towards a radiant future – a future that was regarded
as a scene of everlasting happiness. On the contrary, now the future

---

127 As regards the meaning of a novel when it is compared to significant historical events, it may be worth seeing what Kundera observes on the relationship
between fiction and facts: "L'historiographie écrit l'histoire de la société, non
pas celle de l'homme. C'est pourquoi les événements historiques dont mes
romans parlent sont souvent oubliés par l'historiographie". Milan Kundera, *L'art
du roman*, Paris, Gallimard, 1986, p. 51.

is a desert that Constance and Sophia cross as the final stage of their existence.

Tellingly, the narrator transcodifies Constance's thoughts as he investigates her inner world: "At fifty-one she regarded herself as old. And she was old" (*OWT*, p. 495). If it is true that in 1862 the elder sister was sixteen, towards the end of the nineteenth century – thirty-five years later the world is no longer the same. In 1897 Constance registers her physical failure which reflects a psychological failure, a weakness which would have seemed unthinkable only a few years previously: "She was a rather fragile, small, fat woman, soon out of breath, easily marred" (*OWT*, p. 497). The carefree years when St Luke's Square seemed to contain the whole world are long past – everything has changed. The two sisters now live with the awareness that they have come to the end of their final painful battle against time. On her return to Bursley after thirty years' absence, Sophia discovers another world. She no longer sees things in the same way she did when she was a little child. Now everything appears different, smaller – even the square seems incredibly tiny: "She had expected, of course, to find that the Square had shrunk in size; but, nevertheless, she was startled to see how small it was" (*OWT*, p. 512). Besides the waste of time and the different prospective with respect to the spatial dimension, Sophia surveys the memories of her childhood which, in light of her experiences in Paris, take on a completely new shade of meaning in which the past – the years spent in the house in which she was born – becomes a space of refuge and protection:

> She could remember a winter morning when from the window she had watched the Square under virgin snow in the lamplight, and the Square had been vast [...] These visions of herself seemed *beautiful* to her; her childish existence seemed *beautiful*; the storms and tempests of her girlhood seemed *beautiful*; even the great sterile expanse of tedium when, after giving up a scholastic career, she had served for two years in the shop – even this had a strange charm in her memory (*OWT*, p. 512, corsivi miei).

By downplaying the difficulties of her childhood ("the storms and tempests [...]", Sophia, as a mature woman, observes her years in Bursley as the representation of a beauty that can no longer be recovered and that, in light of her experiences in Paris and her personal disappointments, she exalts in the theatre of her memory. Everything is recovered because, ultimately, Sophia can now look back to that familiar past as the only certainty and, in a sense, the only moment of truth. In the three-times repetition of the adjective *beautiful* may be noted the particular association between the beauty and the topology of the beginning in terms of a radical revision of her life. After her experience in the *ville lumière* where corruption, vice and vulgarity lay hidden beneath the lights and the colours, Sophia discovers another kind of beauty that is not artificial because a product of hard work and the sacrifice of daily life.

From this point of view, her return home allows Sophia to discover another kind of value, that of a moral beauty which, in the end, is what her memories extract from a town that belongs more to the world of the dead than that of the living. It is from this world that Gerald Scales re-emerges nine years after Sophia's departure from Paris. After receiving a telegramme, the woman, still officially Mrs Scales – rushes to Manchester where she discovers that her husband died a few days previously. After learning that Gerald had died of "exhaustion" (*OWT*, p. 579), she asks to see him: "What affected her was that he had once been young, and that he had grown old, and was now dead. *That was all. Youth and vigour had come to that. Youth and vigour always came to that. Everything came to that*" (*OWT*, p. 580, my italics). From the point of view of the narrative structure, it is not exaggerated to say that these words represent the real epilogue of the novel. After observing death on the decayed face of her husband, she suddenly realises that time is the great devourer, the victor of every battle – no youthfulness can possibly oppose the passing of time and no beauty can be a barrier to the wrinkles of time.

Ultimately, *The Old Wives' Tale* is Bennett's attempt to trace the gradual transition from youth to old-age in terms of a silent tragedy, the same tragedy to which he refers in the "Preface" when he writes: "Her case is a tragedy". Tragedy does not only belong to the decrepit old lady observed in the restaurant but to everyone. A few days after the death of Scales, Sophia also suffers the same destiny: "Sophia seemed to be in a kind of coma. The distortion of her handsome face was more marked as time passed" (OWT, p. 587). As Constance nurses her sister in her final hours, they are close together again as they were in their childhood. After only a few months, Constance also dies of pericarditis in a moment during which there is a great discussion regarding a project to unify the group of small towns that make up the Potteries into a single federation: "It was on a muddy day in October that the first great battle for and against Federation was fought in Bursley. Constance was suffering severely from sciatica. She was also suffering from disgust with the modern world" (*OWT*, p. 605).

It is now November 1907 and Constance, who is sixty-one years old, observes the changes with the disgust of a person who can no longer understand the young generation. The fact that her son Cyril does not attend her funeral ("He arrived three days later", *OWT*, p. 619) also confirms the loneliness of her fate in her final days. But before she dies, Constance is unable to stop thinking of her sister as she reflects over her sad destiny: "She frequently thought of Sophia. In spite of the fact that Sophia was dead she still pitied Sophia as a woman whose life had been wasted" (*OWT*, p. 617). In a sense, her regret for her sister indicates the extent to which the two sisters, as they exit from the scene, have been the protagonists of two different kinds of tragedy – Constance the heroine of a domestic tragedy devoid of affection and Sophia the heroine of a romantic tragedy made up of illusions and great sacrifices. For both, time – if intended as a personification as in a medieval morality play – embodies a double role: it is both the implacable destroyer and, paradoxically, the master that finally teaches the vanity of all things. This conclusion may be connected with Sophia's observation over the corpse of her husband: "That was all. Youth and vigour had come to that. Youth and vigour always came to that. Everything came to that" (*OWT*, p. 580). In this sense, the novel may be read as much more than a simple story of the Potteries, but as a great work, a metaphor[128] not only

---

128 The term "metaphor" with reference to *The Old Wives' Tale* is here used in the same sense as David Lodge who underlines how the profound meaning of a narrative work must not be confused with its plot. As Lodge writes: "The import of a narrative is a 'metaphoric' totalization of its meanings, a realization that its ending is the-same-as-but-but-different-from its beginning, but the route by which this goal is reached is a metonymic chain of temporal sequence and cause-and-effect". David Lodge, *Write On: Occasional Essays '65–'85*, London, Secker and Warburg, 1986, p. 198.

of life in its daily unfolding, but also of the extent to which youth and vigour are inextricably linked with old-age and decrepitude[129].

---

129 It goes without saying that old-age is one of the greatest themes of world litera-
     ture. See on this point *De Senectute*, written by Cicero in 44 B.C.

CHAPTER 4 The "Grim Smile" of the Potteries: A Reading of "The Silent Brothers" and "The Death of Simon Fuge"

1. "I propose to amuse myself during August & September by writing a few really good short stories"[130]. When Arnold Bennett wrote these words to his literary agent, he was referring in particular to "The Silent Brothers", a story unjustly neglected by his critics[131]. The years between 1900 and 1914 saw a peak in the popularity of weekly and monthly literary journals in which short stories were published. For a prolific writer like Bennett concerned with the provincial life of the Potteries, short stories were an opportunity to earn money and fame[132]. However, Walter Allen is unjust when he claims that "Bennett was not a natural short-story writer"[133] merely because his stories were accused of being exaggeratedly farcical or pathetically sad. Certainly, his scrupulous attention to detail required a larger canvass than the short story provided. However, in spite of their brevity, his powers of observation, sense of comedy and keen awareness of the tastes of the average reader, confirmed the writer's two-fold social function: to impart a moral

---

130 James Hepburn, *Letters of Arnold Bennett*, 4 vols., London, Oxford University Press, 1968, I, p. 62 (letter dated 26 April 1905). A few months later, (31 October 1905) James Brand Pinker received another letter in which Bennett wrote: "My dear Pinker, I send you by registered book post the three other humorous stories. Of the six, 'The Lion's Share' is the best, and 'The Silent Brothers' the next best" (p. 63).

131 The Silent Brothers", after long negotiation, was published in June 1907 by Chapman and Hall who were willing to pay twenty per cent of the author's rights, a sum which Chatto and Windus had refused Bennett.

132 The story "The Silent Brothers" was sent to *Windsor Magazine* which published it in July 1907, a month after the publication of *The Grim Smile of the Five Towns*.

133 Walter Allen, *Arnold Bennett*, London, Home & Van Thal, 1948, p. 90.

lesson and a knowledge of the ways of the world while cultivating a pleasure for reading.

In this respect, it would be worthwhile recalling H.G. Wells's comments on Bennett's short stories: "'The Grim Smile' is I think your high watermark so far. I've read it and admire and envy a pen so wonderfully under control and now astonishingly expert"[134]. Bennett had, by this time, published eleven novels and a vast number of essays and articles and, in spite of Virginia Woolf's criticism of him as an outdated patriarch and an impediment to those writers who were considered the experimental liberators of modernism, Bennett's works must be recognized for their extraordinarily sensitive evocation of English provincial life. His minute attention towards the structure and technique of the novel derives partly from French literature, particularly Balzac and Maupassant, whereas his inventiveness may be easily traced to the influence of Russian masters such as Turgenev and Tolstoy. As far as English authors are concerned, it would not be too audacious to compare the subtle nuances in Bennett's representation of place to the works of Thomas Hardy and D.H. Lawrence.

As John Lucas rightly notes, "Bennett is *the* novelist of the ordinary"[135]. Indeed, all of the writer's works revolve around common characters whose lives in the Five Towns move slowly and are made up of ordinary habits and conventions naturally exposed to the erosions of time. In his keen and minute attention to literary themes and forms, Bennett has created a literary geography made up not only of romantic realism but also of an acute sensitivity to space and individual destiny.

2. "The Silent Brothers" is a story set in Bursley – the fictional name for the same town in which live the main characters of *The Old Wives' Tale*, (published a year later in 1908). Although they share the same setting, the two works are at opposite poles, not only in terms of length. Whereas the novel is concerned with two sisters, the short story focusses on two brothers. Also, in "The Two Brothers" there is an almost complete absence of description of the environment in contrast

---

134 Harris Wilson, ed., *Arnold Bennett and H.G. Wells. A Record of a Personal and a Literary Friendship*, Urbana, University of Illinois Press, p. 143.

135 John Lucas, *Arnold Bennett: A Study of his Fiction*, London, Methuen, 1974, p. 26, italics in the text.

with the almost excessively lengthy descriptions in *The Old Wives' Tale*, particularly at the beginning of the novel:

> Those two girls, Constance and Sophia Baines, paid no heed to the manifold interest of their situation, of which, indeed, they had never been conscious. They were, for example, established almost precisely on the fifty-third parallel of latitude. A little way to the north of them, in the creases of a hill famous for its religious orgies, rose the river Trent, the calm and characteristic stream of middle England. Somewhat further northwards, in the near neighbourhood of the highest public-house in the realm, rose two lesser rivers, the Dane and the Dove, which, quarrelling in early infancy, turned their backs on each other, and, the one by favour of the Weaver and the other by favour of the Trent, watered between them the whole width of England, and poured themselves respectively into the Irish Sea and the German Ocean. What a county of modest, unnoticed rivers! What a natural, simple county, content to fix its boundaries by these tortuous island brooks, with their comfortable names – Trent, Mease, Dove, Tern, Dane, Mees, Stour, Tame, and even hasty Severn![136]

Like a camera, the focus shifts through a sequence of frames including images within a geographic space and exact latitude (*fifty-third parallel*) before gradually narrowing down from the physical description of rivers, hills and the railway line to the town of Bursley and St Luke's Square where the Baines' shop is located and which the narrator proceeds to describe with a good deal of familiarity. As Bennett comments in his Preface to the novel: "I had lived in the shop and knew it as only a child could know it"[137].

In comparison with *The Old Wives' Tale*, the opening of "The Two Brothers" is altogether different: "John and Robert Hessian[138], brothers and bachelors, dressed in mourning, sat together after supper in the parlour of their house at the bottom of Oldcastle Street, Bursley. Maggie[139], the middle-aged servant, was clearing the

---

136 Arnold Bennett, *The Old Wives' Tale*, Harmondsworth, Penguin, 1983, p. 37.
137 *Ibid.*, p. 33.
138 Names in Bennett's works are never accidental. In this case, the surname *Hessian*, refers both to mathematical calculation which originates from the German language (from Ludwig Otto Hesse), and to the meaning of "hessian" in English: rigidity, on the one hand, and coarseness on the other. These two characteristics are appropriate to the two brothers.
139 Maggie is also the name of the maid in *The Old Wives' Tale*.

table"[140]. In a few lines, the reader is given all the necessary information concerning the protagonists. In contrast with the narrative technique adopted for the opening of *The Old Wives' Tale*, the focus shifts from the particular to the general and from the internal to the external. Furthermore, the spatial references are given only after the stringent and simple description of the protagonists. From a diegetic viewpoint the story is narrated in the third person by an omniscient narrator who controls everything and knows the thoughts of the protagonists:

> "Leave the cloth and the coffee" said John, the elder, "Mr Liversage is coming in".
> "Yes, Mr John", said Maggie.
> "Slate, Maggie", Robert ordered laconically, with a gesture towards the mantelpiece behind him.
> "Yes, Mr Robert", said Maggie (*SB*, p. 34).

The introduction of the two brothers is immediately followed by two concise, dogmatic requests: John, the elder, asks the maid to leave the tablecloth and the coffee on the table as he is expecting a guest, Mr Liversage, while Robert asks Maggie to pass him the slate. It soon becomes clear to the reader that this is the only object through which the two brothers communicate. Indeed, the title of the story already suggests one of its fundamental themes: lack of communication, which in this case means silence:

> Robert took the slate and wrote on it: *"What is Liversage coming about?"*
> And he pushed the slate across the table to John.
> Whereupon John wrote on the slate: *"Don't know. He telephoned me he wanted to see us tonight"*.
> And he pushed back the slate to Robert (*SB*, p. 34, italics in the text).

Yet, this is not the silence of voices since the protagonists are not dumb or incapable of making sounds. Neither, as the narrator informs the reader, was that "singular procedure [...] attributable to deafness on the part of the brothers" (*SB*, p. 34). Rather, the silence is the result of their mutual hostility as a result of a ten-year-old argument which has

---

140   Arnold Bennett, *The Grim Smile of the Five Towns*, Harmondsworth, Penguin, 1946, p. 34. Henceforth all quotations are from this edition indicated in the text as SB followed by page numbers.

forced them into a "self-imposed dumbness" (*SB*, p. 35). Their introduction, however, is marked by the words with which they address a
middle-aged governess whose role, as appears immediately evident, is
to facilitate their non-verbal communication.

All of Bennett's short-stories, from *The Grim Smile of the Five
Towns* to *Tales of the Five Towns* and *The Matador of the Five Towns*[141]–
are largely based on anecdotes, incidents of a particular or peculiar
nature of the private lives of individuals of the Potteries. In this case,
it is the inhabitants of Bursley who manifest an interest in the story
and, in their knowledge of the incident are initially curious spectators
and eventually, with the passing of time, regard the falling out between
the two brothers with tolerance and impartiality, almost as if it were
"a sort of elemental fact of Nature" (*SB*, p. 35). Indeed: "the collective
eye of Bursley is much too large and important to occupy itself with a
single individual" (*SB*, p. 40). Although the story is somewhat banal,
it allows Bennett to express all his irony towards his region of origin
and its inhabitants whose most widespread sentiments are made up of
a "strange compound of pride, obstinacy, unconquerableness, romance,
and stupidity. Yes, stupidity" (*SB*, p. 34). This portrayal may appear
excessively harsh. Yet, to a reader familiar with Bennett's works, such
harsh language to describe the characteristics of the inhabitants of
the Potteries comes as no surprise. In particular, pride – which seems
to be the dominant sentiment of the inhabitants of the Five Towns –
is highlighted in almost all of his works, as, for example in *The Old
Wives' Tale*:

> Happily the inhabitants of the Five Towns in that era were passably *pleased with
> themselves*, and they never even suspected that they were not quite modern and
> quite awake. They thought that the intellectual, the industrial, and the social
> movements had gone about as far as these movements could go, and they were
> *amazed at their own progress*. Instead of being humble and ashamed, they
> actually showed *pride* in their pitiful achievements[142].

---

141   The two collections were published respectively in 1905 and 1912.
142   Bennett, *The Old Wives' Tale*, cit., p. 47 (corsivi miei).

Images of pride and stubbornness also emerge from the pages of *Anna of the Five Towns*[143] in which the young woman is advised to put pride to one side and have the courage to be humble and submissive: " 'But it is quite simple' said Mrs Sutton. 'I cannot tell you anything that you do not know. Cast out *pride*. Cast out *pride* – that is it. Nothing but earthly *pride* prevents you from realising the saving power of Christ. You are afraid, Anna, afraid to be humble. Be brave. It is so simple, so easy. If one will but submit' "[144].

It is precisely the deep-rooted pride of the Hessian brothers which is fully dependant on the local ethos, that prevents them from talking to each other. This self-imposed silence, of which the whole community is aware, even becomes a motive of pride: "[t]he brothers acquired *pride* in it" (*SB*, p. 35, my italics). It is because of their wounded pride that John and Robert have chosen a silence, which is to be traced to their love for the same woman; the twenty-three-year old Annie Emery:

> Each brother had accused the other of underhand and unbrotherly practices in the pursuit of Annie. Each was profoundly hurt by the accusations, and each, in the immense fatuity of his *pride*, had privately sworn to prove his innocence by having nothing more to do with Annie. Such is life! Such is man! Such is the terrible egoism of man! And thus it was that, for the sake of wounded *pride*, John and Robert not only did not speak to one another for ten years, but they spoilt at least one of their lives; and they behaved ignobly to Annie, who would certainly have married either one or the other of them (*SB*, p. 39, corsivi miei).

From an artistic point of view, however, the incident presents some undeniable weaknesses: The protagonists work for the same majolica factory, Roycroft[145], but they have different jobs (John is a foreman

---

143   It must be noted here that Bennett's female protagonists are only passive on the surface. This is true of both Mrs Mary Ann Bott, John and Robert Hessian's sister, and Miss Annie Emery. For an illuminating analysis of another apparently resigned character, that of Anna Tellwright, see Francesco Marroni, "The Paradigm of Negativity in *Anna of the Five Towns*", *Cahiers Victoriens et Edouardiens*, 41 (Avril 1995), pp. 99–120.

144   Arnold Bennett, *Anna of the Five Towns*, Harmondsworth, Penguin, 2001, p. 71 (my italics).

145   Again, this is a fictional name for which Arnold Bennett probably took his cue from the "Moorcraft" factory, famous for the very high standard of its ceramics.

while Robert is a representative). For this reason, they find themselves forced to communicate with each other from time to time, thus suspending their hostilities in the interest of a sort of armistice. As the narrator ironically comments, this forced interruption of their silence is "the sole imperfection in a lovely and otherwise perfect quarrel" (*SB*, p. 35) between two individuals stirred solely by pride, stupidity and habit. The story is pervaded by a bitter irony, a "grim smile" on the part of Bennett who in one of his numerous interventions expresses his scornful judgment of the two brothers affirming that "no one suggested the lunatic asylum" (*SB*, p. 36) for them.

Mr Powell Liversage's visit, which interrupts their habitual encounters, concerns the discovery of the will of their sister, Mrs Mary Ann Bott, the widow of a rich colour merchant. Not even her death, which occurs three months previously, has been able to make them put aside their pride: "Even at the funeral the brothers had scandalised the town by *not speaking* to each other" (*SB*, p. 37, my italics). As a lawyer and old friend of the brothers- and like them a bachelour – he has been named as the legal representative of the inheritance. The will marks a turning point in the lives of the two brothers and, in its impertinence, represents a narrative and legal text the effects of which further the irony of the story:

> This is my will. You are both of you extremely foolish, John and Robert, and I've often told you so. Nobody has ever understood, and nobody ever will understand, why you quarrelled like that over Annie Emery. You are punishing yourselves, but you are punishing her as well, and it isn't fair her waiting all these years. So I give all my estate, no matter what it is, to whichever of you marries Annie. And I hope this will teach you a lesson. You need it more than you need my money. But you must be married within a year of my death. And if the one that marries cares to give five thousand pounds or so to the other, of course there's nothing to prevent him. This is just a hint. And if you don't either of you marry Annie within a year, then I just leave everything I have to Miss Annie Emery (spinster), stationer and fancy-goods dealer, Duck Bank[146], Bursley. She deserves something for her disappointment, and she shall have it. Mr Liversage, solicitor,

---

146 In reality the "Duck Bank" area bears the name "Swan Bank". See M.C. Rintoul, *Dictionary of Real People and Places in Fiction*, London and New York, Routledge, 1993, p. 875.

must kindly be my executor. And I commit my soul to God, hoping for a blessed resurrection. 20th January, 1896. Signed Mary Ann Bott, widow (*SB*, p. 38).

Once again, however, the reading of the final wishes of Mrs Bott, whose intentions can be seen as an attempt to teach the two brothers a lesson, is met with a silence which, in this case, also includes Mr Liversage: "Each was *afraid to speak*, afraid even to meet the eyes of the other two. An *unmajestic silence* followed" (*SB*, p. 39, my italics). Not only, but their silence becomes a strategy to maintain a secret with the addresser of the will herself: As Robert says, addressing himself to Mr Liversage: "Better *not say anything* about this to Miss – to Annie, eh?" (*SB*, p. 39)[147] persisting in his inclination to plan and imagine situations in which things are not said and not manifested. Even when John decides to break the silence at two o'clock in the morning by proposing to toss a coin to decide who will propose to Miss Emery, Robert is unable to answer aloud: "[s]omething stronger even than the desire prevented his tongue from moving" (*SB*, p. 40). The only word he is able to mutter, confusing the two sides of the coin, is "tails".

3. In the second of the four moments which make up the story, Bennett concentrates his irony on the winner of the toss with a simple description of the behaviour of a simple character: the narrative interventions are numerous and particularly amusing in the dramatization of the events that revolve round the figure of John Hessian, who is intent on making up for ten years silence with a woman who "would never be twenty-three again" (*SB*, p. 42). Clumsy and fearful in confronting Miss Annie Emery, the "donkey"[148]– in the hope that the woman will not be at home, begins with the banal though significant comment "I was just passing" (*SB*, p. 41). As the narrator observes, partly explaining the

---

147 The reader is informed by the narrator that their faithful friend has, in fact, already warned Miss Annie Emery: "'I will say nothing' agreed Liversage (infamously and unprofessionally concealing the fact that he had already said something)" (*SB*, p. 39). His figure appears to be dishonest in terms of their friendship from his first entrance in the house when, exploiting his total estrangement to the will, he affirms that "it's not my will. I've had nothing to do with it" (*SB*, p. 38).

148 As the narrator puts it: "I was just passing, the *donkey* in him blundered forth" (p. 41, my italics).

mental lucubration of the character: "You can't tell a woman you've called to make love to her, and when your previous call happens to have been ten years ago, some explanation does seem to be demanded" (*SB*, p. 42). Nevertheless, the intimacy that is established between the couple within the first few minutes seems unnatural even to the most distracted reader. Miss Emery is by no means unprepared for the encounter as she sits in her drawing room where an elegant table has been laid and where, only a quarter of an hour after his entrance, John Hessian feels so much at his ease that he proposes to her. The woman, on her part, reveals no resentment for his shamelessness and makes a sort of pact with the impudent suitor which is also based on silence. In fact, she communicates her agreement through a non-verbal sign by putting white roses onto her hat as if for a Sunday service on condition that no words will pass between them: "In any case, *you mustn't speak to me* coming out of chapel" (*SB*, p. 44, my italics). The exclusion of spoken words, therefore, is suggested by the woman herself, who seems to want to attack John Hessian with his own weapons: everything is then once more reduced to a silence in which, apparently, only the visible counts.

Nothing seems to have changed in the Hessian brothers' house as they consume their Sunday breakfast "in their usual august *silence*" (*SB*, p. 44, my italics) before going to church where, with his focus on John who ridicules the white roses in Miss Annie's hat. Once again, silence is the protagonist of the dinner between the two inhabitants of Bursley who are intently reading two different articles. In his certainty of an imminent Christian union with Annie, it is appropriate that John is reading the *Christian Commonwealth* magazine, while Robert is absorbed in the sports section of the *Signal*, a choice that elicits a comment on the part of the narrator who regrets the fact of reading news about cricket on the day of Our Lord[149]. The truth is that Annie has made the same pact with Robert and, for this reason, both find themselves outside her front door forced to interrupt their silence for the same reason they started it ten years previously. As for what happens once they rush home, the narrator himself adopts a strategy of silence denying the reader the story of their mutual clarification: "The scene was not such as can be decently recounted" (*SB*, p. 49).

---

149   "I regret it" (*SB*, p. 45).

The diegetic development of the story culminates in a comic-grotesque epilogue which, although it leaves something unresolved in the lives of the silent brothers, at the same time reveals the truth about a character who had not been intentionally credible from his first appearance. The words with which the fourth and final movement of the story begins disorient the reader as they are marked by a very confidential tone which unites the two interlocuters and, proleptically, discloses the behaviour of Miss Emery. On a magnificent summer evening in the garden, with the moon in the twilight, to the question that Powell Liversage innocently asks Annie: "But whatever made you do it, dearest?" (*SB*, p. 47), the woman reveals she acted out of revenge. She could not bear the idea that only money could interrupt the silence that had fallen between them. Once again, silence characterises the feelings the lawyer Liversage has for the woman to whom he has become recently engaged: "You see, *I've never breathed a word to them* – about my feelings towards you" (*SB*, p. 48, my italics). It will not be their sister who teaches John and Robert the most important lesson ("I hope this will teach you a lesson", SB, p. 38) but the object of their common desires that, as a result of the rediscovery of the false will, effects a sort of settling of accounts. In contrast with Annie's honest character, seen in her refusal of "vile money" (*SB*, p. 48), Powell's psychological dimension is enclosed in the comment expressed by the narrator who, partly through amusement and partly through bitterness, evidences the meanest aspects of human beings. Although he denies being attached to money for obvious reasons, Mr Liversage's "baser part somewhat regretted that vile twelve thousand or so. (*I must be truthful*)" (*SB*, p. 48, my italics). A characteristic of Bennett's technique, this aside evidences both the superficial character of romanticism or, rather, feelings of love and the ironic detachment with which the narrator observes his characters. Declaring "I must be truthful" on the last page of the story, Bennett takes control of the scene and reaffirms his profound sagacity and knowledge of the vices and virtues of the people of the Potteries.

4. "The Death of Simon Fuge"[150], which is the second last story of the collection *The Grim Smile of The Five Towns*, may be regarded as a

---

150 "The Death of Simon Fuge" is included in Bennett's second collection of short stories, *The Grim Smile of the Five Towns*, which was published in 1907 by

minor masterpiece in Arnold Bennett's canon, as well as one of the best short stories in English[151]. The fact that the art of understatement seems to be at the heart of its plot-construction has led various critics to label it as a Chekhovian[152] story. Indeed, in foregrounding a representation of life in conformity with the principles of realism, Bennett places great emphasis on the fact that people's lives are dominated not so much by causality but by ambiguity and that while they seem to be permanently striving for order, in the end they are only confronted with disorder and mystery. One of the fundamental paradigms of "The Death of Simon Fuge" is, in fact, the unintelligibleness of life, which in this case means the unintelligibleness of an artist's life. Indeed, there is an intriguing episode in the life of the eponymous artist which is one of the themes on which the story is based. Another important element is represented by the contrast between the real truth and what the narrator imagines to be true. "The Death of Simon Fuge" is structured around a series of recurring contrasts which can be encapsulated by the binary opposi-tions reality *vs.* fiction, life *vs.* death, beauty *vs.* ugliness, refinement *vs.* coarseness, authenticity *vs.* prejudice, centre *vs.* periphery and art *vs.*

Chapman and Hall, London. Regarding the story's composition, it may be worthwhile mentioning what Bennett wrote in his journal on the 27th March 1907: "In three days I have written nearly 6,000 words of a long short story called 'The Death of Simon Fuge', not destined for any magazine. I enjoyed writing this more than I have enjoyed writing anything for a long tome. Not to have the fear of the unperceptive stupidity of the magazine public before your eyes is certainly a wonderful release" (Arnold Bennett, *The Journals*, ed. Frank Swimmerton, Harmondsworth, Penguin, 1971, p. 190).

151 See John Wain, *Arnold Bennett*, New York, Columbia University Press, 1967, p. 47; and also John Wain, "Remarks on the Short Story", *Journal of the Short Story in English*, 41 (Autumn 2003), http://jsse.revues.org/index318.html [accessed July 2009].

152 Many critics have underlined Arnold Bennett's debts to Chekhov's art of the short story. As a matter of fact, when he wrote "The Death of Simon Fuge" he had never read a line of the Russian writer – eventually Bennett became a great admirer of Chekhov's narrative genius. See, on this point, John Carey: "[...] his admiration for Chekhov led to publication of Chekhov's short stories in the *New Age*. When the audience of the first performance of *The Cherry Orchard* walked out in disgust, Bennett defended the play's 'daring naturalism'" (John Carey, *The Intellectuals and The Masses. Pride and Prejudice among the Literary Intel-ligentsia 1880–1939*, London and Boston, Faber and Faber, 1992, p. 156).

industry. This latter point certainly applies to Simon Fuge, an inspired painter whose art has been barely recognized by the Pottery people among whom he has lived all his life.

From a diegetic angle, the story is narrated by the main protagonist, Mr Loring, a ceramics expert from London who is visiting the Potteries for the first time. Because of his intellectually refined approach to reality, Loring displays a prejudice and misconception of its social context which prevent him from going beyond the limits of his own world and only make him see the ugliness and vulgarity of the Five Towns. This deep-seated conviction conditions Loring's ideological approach to the Potteries and gives a peculiar slant to his vision even before his arrival. Indeed, as Margaret Drabble has rightly observed, in this story "[t]he Five Towns is seen by Bennett for the first time from outside, through the eyes of an outsider. He sees how it strikes a Londoner, and his observations have the mixture of love and recoil that so many exiles feel for their native land"[153]. Loring's reaction toward the townscape of the Potteries is significant: on his arrival at Knype he expresses a sense of revulsion at the scenes before him:

> Well, my impressions of the platform of Knype station were unfavourable. There was dirt in the air; I could feel it at once on my skin. And the scene was shabby, undignified, and rude. I use the word 'rude' in all its senses. What I saw was a pushing, exclamatory, ill-dressed, determined crowd, each member of which was bent on the realization of his own desires by the least ceremonious means. If an item of this throng wished to get past me, he made me instantly aware of his wish by abruptly changing my position in infinite space; it was not possible to misconstrue his meaning. So much crude force and naked will-to-live I had not before set eyes on. In truth, I felt myself to be a very brittle, delicate bit of intellectual machinery in the midst of all these physical manifestations. Yet I am a tallish man, and these potters appeared to me to be undersized, and somewhat thin too! But what elbows! What glaring egoistic eyes! What terrible decisiveness in action![154]

153 Margaret Drabble, *Arnold Bennett. A Biography*, London, Weidenfeld and Nicolson, 1974, p. 144.

154 Arnold Bennett, "The Death of Simon Fuge", in *The Grim Smile of the Five Towns*, Harmondsworth, Penguin, 1946, p. 137. All subsequent quotations will be given in the text as *DSF* followed by page numbers.

The dominant note of the passage is that of an industrial world strongly marked by egoistic drives which leave no room for unselfish feelings, elegance and beauty. In addition to this pervading sense of vulgarity and filth, there is a most evident representation of a context characterized by a Darwinian struggle for life which lowers the monotonous existence of the inhabitants of the Potteries to the level of beasts. Far away from the sophistication and finesse of London life, Loring sees around him only rude and ill-mannered people. This contrast between the British Museum expert and the Potteries is rendered in a very precise way on a linguistic level. On the one hand, there is a major lexical set which presents Knype in its full ugliness by means of adjectives such as *unfavourable, shabby, undignified, rude, ill-dressed, crude, naked,* and *egoistic.* On the other, the narrating voice cannot help defining himself in terms of weakness and fragility: *brittle* and *delicate* are the adjectives through which he expresses his feeling of helplessness before the industrial context he is about to visit.

5. An important structuring element of the story is the title itself since it works on at least three levels. On a first level, it triggers what, in a Barthesian sense[155], is defined as the hermeneutical code. Indeed, the reader cannot help refraining from posing some very obvious questions: Who is Simon Fuge? Why is his death so central to the meaning of the story? What kind of link is established between Simon Fuge and his death? On a second level, it has a significance which bears on the diegetic development of the story: "The Death of Simon Fuge" seems to be the caption of the obituary that will catch Loring's eye during his train journey to the industrial towns. From a literary point of view, the title is clear, concise and informative; it does not stimulate our curiosity simply because the artist's death is a given, something which has already happened and not a consequence of something which is part of a detective story — for there is no detection in "The Death of Simon

---

155   See Roland Barthes, *S/Z*, Paris, Editions du Seuil, 1970, pp. 25–27. In particular, Barthes observes: "L'inventaire du code herméneutique consistera à distinguer les différents termes (formels), au gré desquels une énigme se centre, se pose, se formule, puis se retarde et enfin se dévoile" (p. 26). With respect to this formulation, it can be maintained that the title of Bennett's short story poses an enigma to the reader.

Fuge". Finally, there is another level which, linguistically speaking, connects the title with the opening of the story:

> It was in the train that I learnt of his death. Although a very greedy eater of lite-rature, I can only enjoy reading when I have little time for reading. Give me three hours of absolute leisure, with nothing to do but read, and I instantly become almost incapable of the act. So it is always on railway journeys, and so it was that evening. I was in the middle of Wordsworth's *Excursion*; I positively gloated over it, won-dering why I should have allowed a mere rumour that it was dull to prevent me from consuming it earlier in my life. But do you suppose I could continue with Wordsworth in the train? I could not (DSF, p. 133).

The story opens *in medias res*, with an anaphoric reference to the title in the syntagm: *his death*, which, as becomes immediately apparent, is the death of Simon Fuge. However, this passage is also important since it gra-dually shifts the focus from the title (Fuge's death) to the man in the train who, as we realize, is the only real protagonist of the story, a character whose behavioural code is strongly dependent on his London experiences.

Considered from a psychological angle, it is all too evident that Simon Fuge, the artist and the man, is a pretext for Loring's self-investigation into his own life and his role in a changing society. In fact, the narrating voice pays no attention whatsoever to Fuge's life and works. Rather, what he is anxious to communicate is his own world-view. Indeed, from what is revealed, the reader may easily infer that he regards himself as an intellectual imbued with romantic aspirations and a consuming desire for self-affirmation. Not surprisingly, the expli-cit and reiterated references to Wordsworth is an indicator of his way of interpreting the world: Wordsworth stands not only for poetry and spirituality and intimacy with nature, but also for the art of walking in a beautiful landscape. This romantic evocation clearly establishes a conflicting relationship with the railway world whose noisy presence and industrial valence are the sheer negation of an aesthetic interpre-tation of life and its spiritual and epiphanic manifestations. Therefore, it is no surprise that, after confessing that he is "positively gloat[ing]" over Wordsworth's *Excursion*, he is ready to give up his reading since the very fact that he is reading it on a train would be an offence to

Wordsworth's art and sanctity[156]. The consequence of Loring's decision is that he resorts to reading a newspaper, which he believes to be the correct thing to do when travelling in a train compartment:

> The second thing that I saw in the *Gazette* [...] was the death of Simone Fuge. There was nearly a column about it, signed with initials, and the subheading of the article ran, 'Sudden death of a great painter'. That was characteristic of the *Gazette*. That Simon Fuge was indeed a great painter is now admitted by most dilettantes, though denied by a few. But to the great public he was just a medium name (*DSF*, p. 134).

After describing in some detail his intellectual frame of mind, Loring makes the casual discovery of the death of Simon Fuge, which is precisely the information proleptically conveyed to the reader in the very first sentence of the story. Coincidentally, Simon Fuge was born in the Potteries which is precisely where the narrator is going for the first time in order to express his appraisal on "some huge slip-decorated dishes" (*DSF*, p. 139). In his imagination, the industrial area is an alien world and a sheer negation of art and he is convinced that dirt and smoking chimneys are the sole dominant elements in that culturally backward area of England. As a consequence, he sees the opposition

---

156 Here the reference to the Romantic poet is definitely autobiographical. In fact, it is well known that William Wordsworth was one of Bennett's most loved poets. This is also confirmed by many passages from his *Journals*: "*Saturday, 5 October [1907]* — Curious example of wit in Wordsworth; I should imagine it to be rather rare: the description of the old pack of cards in the first book of *The Prelude*, pp. 17–18 of the Temple Classics edition. I am now reading *The Prelude* with intense pleasure. I have abandoned several other books in order to read it" (*Journals*, cit., p. 222). Another entry on the 30th May 1908: "I have had great joy in Mr. Nowell Charles Smith's new and comprehensive edition of Wordsworth, published by Methuen in three volumes as majestic as Wordsworth himself at his most pontifical [...] Personally, I became a member of the order of Wordsworthians in the historic year 1891, when Matthew Arnold's Selections were issued to the public at the price of half a crown. I suppose that Matthew Arnold and Sir Leslie Stephen were the two sanest Wordsworthians of us all. And Matthew Arnold put Wordsworth above all modern poets except Dante, Shakespeare, Goethe, Milton, and Molière. The test of a Worthsworthian is the ability to read with pleasure every line that the poet wrote" (Arnold Bennett, *Books and Persons 1926–1931*, ed. Andrew Mylett, London and Hamden, CT, Archon Books, 1974, pp. 26–27).

between the refinement and beauty of his London life and the coarse and meaningless existence characterizing the Potteries. As a result, the emerging opposition is that between the centre (London, the British Museum, Bloomsbury) and the periphery (industry, slums and the negation of culture and art).

It is evident that Loring is about to explore this new reality with a great deal of prejudice the effect of which makes him particularly unable to pierce the surface of that reality:

> My knowledge of industrial districts amounted to nothing. Born in Devonshire, educated at Cambridge, and fulfilling my destiny as curator of a certain department of antiquities at the British Museum, I had never been brought into contact with the vast constructive material activities of Lancashire, Yorkshire, and Staffordshire. I had but passed through them occasionally on my way to Scotland, scorning their necessary grime with the perhaps too facile disdain of the clean-faced southerner, who is apt to forget that coal cannot walk up unaided out of the mine, and that the basin in which he washes his beautiful purity can only be manufactured amid conditions highly repellent (*DSF*, pp. 136–137).

The narrating voice, on the contrary, has by no means a monologic approach to industrialization. As is clearly expressed in the passage, he is fully aware that the dirt and smoke of the Potteries are the price that society must pay in order to have heating systems, refinement and beauty. As a matter of fact, Loring's words testify to an ambivalent attitude which is an anticipation of a more general revision culminating in the demise of his prejudice and preconceptions. At the same time, it is worthwhile underlining that the only person with whom he has been already in contact, Mr Brindley, seems to have subscribed to his prejudiced opinion: "[…] he was a man; he was a very tonic dose. I thought it would be safer to assume that he knew everything, and that the British Museum knew very little. Yet at the British Museum he had been quite different, quite deferential and rather timid. Still, I liked him. I liked his eyes" (*DSF*, p. 142). What is evident here is that, after his very first meeting with Brindley, the narrator starts revising his ideas on the man as well as the environment in which he lived. Thus, the transition from prejudice to authenticity also involves a different interpretation of

Simon Fuge's native region[157]. In addition to establishing an immediate dialogue with Brindley, Loring soon discovers that their own personal taste on such a matter as tobacco was extraordinarily similar – this level of complicity activates a sequence of responses in Loring's mind which go far beyond the professional sphere:

> 'You may pay as much as you like, but you can never buy cigarettes as good as I can make out of an ounce of fresh B.D.V. tobacco. Can you roll one?' I had to admit that I could not, I who in Bloomsbury was accepted as an authority on cigarettes as well as on porcelain. 'I'll roll you one, and you shall try it.'
>
> He did so.
>
> I gathered from his solemnity that cigarettes counted in the life of Mr Brindley. He could not take cigarettes other than seriously. The worst of it was that he was quite right. The cigarette which he constructed for me out of his wretched B.D.V. tobacco was adorable, and I have made my own cigarettes ever since (*DSF*, pp. 140–141).

Although this apparently mundane level of exchange of knowledge on the culture of tobacco and cigarettes is intended to convey a reciprocal and gendered feeling of sympathy between Loring and Brindley, the oblique message that the reader derives from the above passage is very clear: the narrator is experiencing the transition from London to the Potteries as a form of education. In this sense, the B.D.V. episode can be interpreted as a metaphor since it evinces a reversal of roles between the two men: Loring the expert is transformed into Loring the learner ("[…] I have made my own cigarettes ever since"). In many respects, considered from the perspective of the narrating voice (*now*), it seems obvious that the tobacco lesson from Brindley (*then*) has resisted the test of time and modified the narrator's habits for good. This is only a

---

157 In his perceptive analysis of *Anna the Five Towns*, Francesco Marroni observes that, after the narrator's initial rejection of the Five Towns and their possibility of stimulating romance, "the disjunction between the Potteries and the world of romance (the only world that deserves narration) is soon overturned when an explicit authorial commentary establishes the supremacy of romance even in the seemingly dull and unpoetic universe of the Five Towns" (Francesco Marroni, "The Paradigm of Negativity in *Anna of the Five Towns*", *Cahiers Victoriens and Edouardiens*, 41 (Avril 1995), p. 104).

minor aspect of a more general change of attitude towards the life and people of the Potteries[158].

In this episode, as in other episodes of the narration, Simon Fuge's presence remains peripheral and his figure never succeeds in occupying a central place in the story. Another interesting aspect of Loring's mental transformation concerns his response to the interiors of Mr Brindley's house. Indeed, what he expected to see was a very provincial house with no signs of culture or art within its domestic space. After a first glance, however, all these negative terms will be discarded, since his practical and direct contact with Mr Brindley's domestic life reveals quite a different reality to that which Mr Loring anticipated. It is important to show how Loring's narration conveys to the reader the precise moment in which he discovers that nothing is similar to what he had construed. The sharp contrast between the outside and inside of the house is an integral part of Loring's shock:

> We sat down. The room was lighted by four candles, on the table. I am rather short-sighted, and so I did not immediately notice that there were low book-cases all round the walls. Why the presence of these book-cases should have caused me a certain astonishment I do not know, but it did. I thought of Knype station, and the scenery, and then the other little station, and the desert of pots and cinders, and the mud in the road and on the pavement and in the hall, and the baby-linen in the bathroom, and three children all down with mumps, and Mr Brindley's cap and knickerbockers and cigarettes; and somehow the books — I soon saw there were at least a thousand of them, and not circulating-library books, either, but *books* — well, they administered a little shock to me (*DSF*, pp. 144–145).

This amounts to a sort of oblique confession of Loring's failure to immediately understand the positive meanings below the surface of the industrial world which had so aroused his revulsion and cultural rejection. Clearly, his mental construction of an ugly and unsophisticated world goes hand in hand with his anti-industrial prejudice. The Five Towns are more than a townscape characterized by an unremitting

---

158   See Linda R. Anderson, *Bennett, Wells and Conrad: Narrative in Transition*, New York, St Martin's Press, 1988, pp. 53–66. On the theme of education, she acutely notes: "The fact that culture is able to survive in the Five Towns is surprising and Loring's astonishment is not only a part of the educative process which he undergoes there but a response in which we also share" (*DSF*, p. 61).

struggle for life — they are a place where such a good man as Mr Brindley was born and has been living his fully-fledged intellectual life. Somewhat paradoxically, his desire to have an ampler knowledge of Fuge's role in that place is a direct consequence of his revised perspective of the Potteries. The "little shock" the narrator is referring to is related to this change in interpretatation which involves everything and everyone in that place, including the role of the artist in the Potteries.

6. In placing emphasis on Simon Fuge's experience of social marginality in the community of his birth-place, Bennett manifests an anxious desire to explore the role of the artist in the first decades of the twentieth century[159]. The last page of the story shows how powerfully Loring's voice still defends the value of Fuge's art, despite the general suspicion about his life and, even more, the hesitation of such people as Mr Brindley with respect to the recognition of Fuge's mastery in painting. The narrating voice is quite unable to understand why the prevailing position of the people of the Potteries is marked by indifference, if not hostility, towards their fellow townsman. This would have been justified if the Five Towns had been a sort of aesthetic wasteland — which is not the case, as his direct contact with this world has proven. John Lucas's words rightly evidence the emergence of this awareness on Mr Loring's part: "Much of 'The Death of Simon Fuge' is about Loring's gradual realization that for all the outward appearance of meanness and dirt, the Five Towns are not the haunts of barbarians"[160].

Therefore, after having discovered that there is no dissonance between art and the Potteries, it seems even more urgent to Loring that

---

159 See on this point, Tania Zulli, "L'alienazione dell'artista in 'The Death of Simon Fuge'", *Merope*, X, 24 (May 1998), pp. 17–28. With respect to Bennett's relationship with coeval art, it may be interesting to quote what John Carey writes, after underlining that Bennett's taste for literature was very modern and advanced (he defended T. S. Eliot and Joyce): "On painting, Bennett's views were likewise modern, unaffected and unafraid. The Post-Impressionist Exhibition of November 1910, which gave London its first sight of Cézanne, Van Gogh, Gauguin, Vuillard and Matisse, reduced critics and public alike to splutters and guffaws. But Bennett came out firmly on the side of the artists [...]" (Carey, *op. cit.*, p. 157).

160 John Lucas, *Arnold Bennett: A Study of His Fiction*, London, Methuen, 1974, p. 92.

his architect friend take the side of Fuge's art. By all events, the diegetic organization of the story will show, at the very end of his stay in Bursley, that his reiterated efforts have proved unsuccessful:

> 'He was a great artist. And this is his native district. Surely you ought to be proud of him!'
>
> 'He may have been a great artist,' said Mr Brindley, 'or he may not. But for us he was simply a man who came of a family that had a bad reputation for talking too much and acting the goat!'
>
> 'Well,' I said, 'we shall see — in fifty years.'
>
> 'That's just what we shan't,' said he. 'We shall be where Simon Fuge is — dead! However, perhaps we are proud of him. But you don't expect us to show it, do you? That's not our style.'
>
> He performed the quasi-winking phenomenon with his eyes. It was his final exhibition of it to me.
>
> 'A strange place!' I reflected, as I ate my dinner in the dining-car, with the pressure of Mr Brindley's steely clasp still affecting my right hand, and the rich, honest cordiality of his *au revoir* in my heart. 'A place that is passing strange!' (*DSF*, p. 187).

After revising his attitude towards the axiological horizon of the Potteries, the narrator convinces himself that Simon Fuge cannot help being fully accepted and appreciated by the people of his birthplace whose artistic sensibility and aesthetic point of view he has experienced during his stay. Nevertheless, as the above quotation evidences, even such a learned and fairly bookish person as Brindley seems far too reticent to recognize Fuge's art. As a consequence, Loring's farewell to his new friend is imbued with baffling disappointment simply because he would have imagined a more enthusiastic response from Brindley to his wish to reassess Fuge's art. In this sense, such a peremptory opinion as "he was a great artist" (*DSF*, p. 187) voiced by Loring, finds a paradigmatic counterpart in Brindley's hesitation and linguistic encoding: "he may have been a great artist" (*DSF*, p. 187), which involves the idea that Fuge never fully, and convincingly, developed his potential imaginative powers as an artist in the Potteries. And here it may be interesting to note that unlike his fictional painter, Bennett became the great narrator of the Potteries without ever abandoning an ambivalent reading of this industrial area from a moral and artistic point of view.

Of course, Bennett is not Loring, whose manner of interpreting the Potteries is greatly conditioned by his mystifying approach[161]. On another level, Loring's conception of Fuge's life is significantly influenced by his romantic predilections – Wordsworth is still in his mind when he starts to imagine that the artist celebrated in the obituary came from the Potteries where an anecdote imbued with romance had occurred many years before, when Fuge was only a green artist full of great expectations. The enigma Loring wants to unveil concerns a night on a lake which the artist had spent with two local beauties. This romantic tale, narrated by the artist himself, triggers in Loring's imagination a sequence of responses culminating in a romance whose main protagonist is Fuge and two girls whose subsequent life Loring is eager to investigate. According to the artist's narration, this can be defined *the* romance around which Fuge's life has been constructed: "There was a special reference to one of Fuge's most dramatic recitals – a narration of a night spent in a boat on Ilam Lake with two beautiful girls, sisters, natives of the Five Towns, where Fuge was born. Said the obituarist: 'Those two wonderful creatures who played so large a part in Simon Fuge's life'" (*DSF*, p. 135).

In many respects, the obituary is at the origin of the enigma because, after reading the episode of a night in a boat on Ilam Lake, Loring begins to construe his own image of the painter: "[...] Yes, his was a romantic figure, the figure of one to whom everyday, every hour of the day, was coloured by the violence of his passion for existence"

---

161 It is well known that, in Arnold Kettle's view, one of the limitations of Bennett's fiction is that he is unable to fully represent social change. On *The Old Wives's Tale* (1908), one of the most ambitious novels written by Arnold Bennett, Kettle observes: "What I am suggesting is that a novelist must have a really rich imaginative understanding of anything that he writes about and that if his subject involves, as Arnold Bennett's did, a sense of broad social change and development, the novelist's own understanding of these issues is most relevant" (Arnold Kettle, *An Introduction to the English Novel*, London, Hutchinson, 1972, Vol. II, p. 81). Being a short story, "The Death of Simon Fuge" is not planned to dramatise social change, but Kettle's criticism has no bearing on this story precisely because the different attitudes in the assessment of Fuge's art implies the way social change is modifying what Raymond Williams defines as a "structure of feeling" (Raymond Williams, *The Country and the City*, London, Chatto and Windus, 1973, p. 298).

(*DSF*, pp. 135–136). What is more, Loring draws on this episode in order to create his own version of Fuge's early life in the Potteries and, as a result, his mind becomes monopolized by this romanticizing drive:

> Surely – Simon Fuge had obviously been a man whose emotional susceptibility and virile impulsiveness must have opened the door for him to multifarious amours – but surely he had not made himself indispensable to both sisters simultaneously. Surely even he had not so far forgotten that Ilam Lake was in the middle of a country called England [...]
>
> I wondered where Ilam Lake was. I knew merely that it lay somewhere in the environs of the Five Towns. What put fuel on the fire of my interest in the private affairs of the dead painter was the slightly curious coincidence that on the evening of the news of his death I should be travelling to the Five Towns – and for the first time in my life (*DSF*, p. 136).

At this point, another aspect of the educative process in Loring's mind is represented by a final and traumatic awareness: the romance which Fuge had narrated of the two sisters on Ilam Lake was by no means based on reality. What the porcelain expert discovers is only an anti-romance which collides with Fuge's version of events. Kenneth Young well summarizes the nature of this discovery: "Loring meets the two subjects of Fuge's romantic anecdotes – one now a barmaid, another the wife of a rich manufacturer who certainly remembers Fuge on the lake: he talked about neckties and his cold feet and they were back home from the lake by 11 p.m. – so much for the all night outing"[162]. The binary opposition reality *vs.* fiction proves that Fuge was on the side of fiction – his imagination created a romance out of an unexciting night on the lake[163].

---

162 Kenneth Young, *Arnold Bennett*, Harlow, Longman (for the British Council), 1975, p. 21.

163 A truly anti-romantic version of the night on the lake is offered to Loring by Annie Brett's younger sister, now Mrs Colclough:
"'Yes', Mrs Colclough resumed, in a lower, more confidential tone, to the accompaniment of the music. 'You see, there was a whole party of us there, and Mr Fuge was staying at the hotel and of course he knew several of us'.
'And he took you out in a boat?'
'Me and Annie? Yes. Just as it was getting dusk he came up to us and asked if we'd go for a row [...] 'He said the greatest worry in his life had always been neckties [...] I assure you he kept on talking about neckties. I assure you, Mr Loring, I went to sleep – at least I dozed – and when I woke up he was still talking about

As an artist imbued with transforming powers, Fuge has transformed a mundane and meaningless episode into a romantic anecdote which, on close investigation, turns out to be not only a story devoid of truth, but also a fictional recreation the main protagonists of which are by no means such extraordinarily charming girls as the narration implies. When Loring and Mr Brindley go to visit a pub called 'The Tiger', he has the possibility of meeting one of the sisters of the episode, Annie Brett, now a woman of forty: "She was just a little ample, with broad shoulders and a large head [...] As for her face, there were crow's-feet, and a mole (which had selected with infinite skill a site on her chin), and a general degeneracy of complexion" (*DSF*, p. 165). Not only is Annie Brett decidedly unpoetic, but she dismantles every aspect of Fuge's romance: "The least romantic of persons, she had yet felt romance [...] I sought in her face the soft remains of youthfulness. *I invented* languishing poses in the boat. My imagination was equal to the task of seeing her as Simon Fuge saw her" (*DSF*, pp. 169–170, italics mine).

Loring's identification with the artist from the Potteries is an indication of his persistently romantic imagination, even though nothing exceptionally meaningful may be derived from the episode which, according to Annie Brett, now lies wholly in the territory of forgetfulness. "For Loring, Fuge was an artist of genius. But for Brindley and his friends Fuge was a boaster, a loudmouth and a deserter. Besides, he hasn't any relevance to their lives, he isn't materially important"[164]. Thus, the enigma of the two beautiful sisters (what happened that night on the lake? What kind of incidence did the episode have on Fuge's art?) is actually a non-enigma: there is nothing to be discovered just as there is nothing to be revealed to the reader. Although, artistically speaking, Fuge remains an important painter for Loring[165], it goes without

---

neckties. But then his feet began to get cold. I suppose it was because they were wet. The way he grumbled about his feet being cold! [...]' " (*DSF*, pp. 178–179).

164 Lucas, *op. cit.*, pp. 93–94.

165 See Loring's revealing response to a picture by Fuge he sees in the Wedgwood Institution – an old institution which included also a public library, a reading room and a museum: "[...] there was the little picture by Simon Fuge [...] It was a painting, unfinished, of a girl standing at the door and evidently hesitating whether to open the door or not: a very young girl, very thin, with long legs in black stockings, and short, white, untidy frock [...] The face was an infant's face,

saying that his return to London is characterized by a different image of the painter whose life is now as unromantic as it may be. In the light of this revelation it is easy to conclude that the narrator himself is a different person with many doubts as to the role of the artist which, from an aesthetic perspective, make him more aware of the ambiguities and oscillations implied in the interpretative process of biographies and works of art.

---

utterly innocent; and yet Simon Fuge had somehow caught in that face a glimpse of all the future of the woman that the girl was to be, he had displayed with exquisite insolence the essential naughtiness of his vision of things. The thing was not much more than a sketch; it was a happy accident, perhaps, in some day's work of Simon Fuge's. But it was genius. When once you had yielded to it, there was no other picture in the room. It killed everything else" (*DSF*, pp. 161–162)

CHAPTER 5 *Accident*: an adventure and its romantic variations

1. Towards the end of the nineteenth-century, while he was attempting to formulate a new aesthetics for the novel, Bennett declared his total adherence to the narrative methods of the French realist tradition. In his journal on February 1st 1898, he cites Flaubert, the Goncourts brothers and Maupassant[166], to whom he recognises the great merit of having abandoned the techniques of traditional fiction. As John Lucas writes, "[Bennett] was a professed admirer of the Goncourts and Maupassant"[167]. At the same time as he underlined the importance of the French realist novel, Bennett also praised the innovations of the Russian masters. Precisely one year later on January 3 1899, he noted again in his journals: "The achievements of the finest French writers, with Turgenev and Tolstoy, have set a standard for all coming masters of fiction"[168]. It is particularly revealing that Bennett makes no mention in his journals of the great Nineteenth-Century English novelists or the figures of the so-called American Renaissance such as Melville, Hawthorne e Thoreau[169].

From the point of view of his investigation into the novel form, therefore, Bennett was looking beyond England in the apparent attempt to free himself from the literature and culture of his formative years. In doing so, he was clearly seeking to define his role as a writer within the European novel tradition in a transnational and transcultural prospective[170].

---

166 Bennett, *The Journals*, cit., p. 45.
167 Lucas, *op. cit.*, p. 15.
168 *Ibid.*, p. 54.
169 See F. O. Matthiessen, *American Renaissance: Art and Expression in the Age of Emerson and Whitman*, London/ Oxford/New York, Oxford University Press, 1974; first ed. 1941.
170 On the polemical positions against Bennett see Peter Keating: "The carefully plotted phases of life, detailed description of environments and physical states, distanced narrative tone, and the conditioning effects of family life in Bennett's

Nevertheless, one of the first entries in his *Journals*, on 15 October 1896, appears to suggest an approach antithetical to the aesthetics of realism: "Essential characteristic of the really great novelist: a Christ-like all-embracing compassion"[171]. This phrase conveys the idea of *sympathy*, a word that has no place in the vocabulary of the new realist novel with its emphasis on narrative distance. Thus, his focus was on the past, at least from a moral and psychological point of view. The theme of sympathy, which was so important to George Eliot's vision, is a clear indication that Bennett is referring to an implicit and pervasive literary presence associated with romanticism.

As she makes clear in both her letters and epigraphs to her novels, George Eliot derives her vision of religious sympathy not so much from Auguste Comte, as from William Wordsworth[172]. who was the first Romantic poet at the beginning of the nineteenth century, to assert the importance of identifying with the pain and tragedy of others as a response to "the dreary intercourse of daily life"[173], and the social and moral degradation brought about by the industrial revolution and mass migration from the country to the manufacturing towns and cities. It was Wordsworth who provided an ulterior motive for reflection with regard to the future of the novel in terms of its profound exploration of the human passions. Thus, for Bennett also, the novel must never disregard the Christian values of compassion and piety which allow human beings moments of nobility and solidarity. He recognised the extent to

---

fiction proclaim an inescapable debt to France. It was qualities such as these that fuelled Woolf's charge against Bennett of insensitive materialism and helped justify Lawrence's telling dismissal as 'an old imitator' ". Keating, *The Haunted Study: A Social History of the English Novel 1875–1914*, cit., p. 117.

171   Bennett, *The Journals*, cit., p. 24.

172   The topic is dealt with in detail in Francesco Marroni, *La verità difficile: uno studio sui romanzi di George Eliot*, Bologna, Pàtron, 1980, pp. p. 93–94 e pp. 181–187. See also Lilian Haddakin on the importance of Wordsworth for the memory: "She is Wordsworthian also in her insistence on the great power of memory to help the working of the affections and to bind life of the individual to unity". Lilian Haddakin, "Silas Marner", in *Critical Essays on George Eliot*, ed. Barbara Hardy, London, Routledge and Kegan Paul, 1970, p. 67.

173   William Wordsworth, "Lines Composed a Few Miles above Tintern Abbey", *The Poems*, ed. John O. Hayden, 2 Voll., Harmondsworth, Penguin, 1977, I, p. 361 (line 131).

which such a semantic universe is poetically embodied by Wordsworth who, more than any other romantic poet, celebrates man's capacity to experience moments of intense communion.

2. Bennett evidences the importance of Wordsworth's influence at various points in his journals. In spite of this, criticism of Bennett's works never takes Wordsworth into consideration to the extent of giving justice to his moral and aesthetic influence. In spite of the recognition on the part of some critics that Bennett's realism also includes the idea of sympathy, they inevitably refer to Victorian authors without mentioning the sources suggested by Bennett himself. For example, in her oft-cited *Bennett, Wells and Conrad. Narrative in Transition* (1988), Linda R. Anderson underlines that Bennett derived the theme of compassion from Victorian writers without mentioning its romantic origin: "Like many of the Victorian writers of whom he was so critical, Bennett gave the term 'sympathy' special importance in his critical vocabulary"[174]. Anderson simply refers to the quality of "sympathy" without specifying that the term comes, not from the Victorians, but from Wordsworth. Even authors such as George Eliot, Elizabeth Gaskell, Dickens and Trollope, who drew on Wordsworth's poetics for their narrative ideas and ethical orientations, all openly acknowledged the importance of his influence. As Stephen Gill has justly observed: "Wordsworth's achievement served both as a validating authority for their own projects and as a model for artistic possibilities. In their works many of Wordsworth's deepest concern were explored afresh and the force of his poetic formulations renewed"[175]. However, the absence of direct or indirect references to Wordsworth in Anderson's study is astonishing. For while the critic deals with the effects produced by compassion, he never refers to its real source:

> The notion of sympathy provided Bennett with the means of transmuting the passive indifference of the realist writer towards his material into a general principle of connection. In this way he could give a moral emphasis to the realists' belief that all aspects of life could be made the subject of art[176].

---

174 Anderson, *op. cit.*, p. 52.
175 Stephen Gill, *Wordsworth and the Victorians*, Oxford and New York, Oxford University Press/Clarendon Press, 2001, p. 117.
176 Anderson, *op. cit.*, p. 52.

Obviously, in view of the ideals of totality propounded by French authors, Bennett's adherence to late nineteenth-century realism meant above all adherence to a conception of the novel that should not be limited in terms of its themes. Nevertheless, for Bennett, the idea that the novel should deal with the crudest and most unpleasant aspects of reality clashed with his rejection of exaggerated representations of the most vulgar and inhuman aspects of society. He categorically refuted the concept of Zola's "human beast", for example. Moreover, he posed limitations on realism when he declared – almost as if to underline his fidelity to Wordsworth's poetics – that he did not believe that the vulgar, the obscene and crude could be aesthetically valid in creating a novel form that could transcend Victorian models:

> What the artist has to grasp is that there is no such thing as ugliness in the world. This I believe to be true, but perhaps the saying would sound less difficult in another form: All ugliness has an aspect of beauty. The business of the artist is to find that aspect[177].

In reality, the quotation contains in synthesis a great deal of what constitutes Bennett's aesthetics. For the writer undoubtedly rejects the vulgarity of common sexuality, considering Zola's naturalist novels to be a sort of narrative perversion that has little to do with the great English literary tradition and, above all, with the sense of decency and decorum that has always characterised English artistic exploration. Again, in his criticism of naturalist diction may be seen the influence of Wordsworth who had placed such a central importance on the use of a language capable of interpreting reality without the exaggerations and visionary perversions of his friend Coleridge.

One aspect of Bennett's thought which must be underlined concerns his ability to exert such a powerful control over his texts that he achieves a dynamic and credible representation of reality at every narrative level. In a letter to George Sturt on 4 November 1907, Bennett, who was now fifty years-old, observed that his philosophical influences have been "nothing but Marcus Aurelius & Christ assimilated and excreted by me in suitable form"[178]. In effect, the writer confesses to elaborating

---

177 Bennett, *The Journals*, p. 54.
178 Hepburn, *Letters of Arnold Bennett*, cit., II vol., p. 220.

in his mind the stoic philosophy of Marcus Aurelius and relating it to a Christian, or Christological view of life. In other words, in the Heraclitan flow of all things and the transience of human passions, Bennett recognises the great truths that allow him to avoid exaggeration in both euphoric and dysphoric terms. This essentially disenchanted approach, however, does not detract from Bennett's sympathetic view of life as the writer enervates his literary productions with a vision of the world which is far from simplistic. For Bennett cannot be seen as a mere imitator of French derived models but rather, a narrator who creates a novel form in which sensationalistic elements are attenuated in the light of Marcus Aurelius' stoic relativism. In many ways, Bennett's experience as a critic and reviewer led him to the realisation that one of the most important aspects of literature concerns the function of the author who is always axiomatically invested with authority[179].

Unfortunately, critical tradition has generally ignored the multiple suggestions and influences at the heart of Bennett's fiction and too often regarded the author as simply being more concerned with the literary marketplace than artistic exploration. One particular definition of Bennett, which appears to encapsulate the alternating poles of the writer's theories, is the title of Walter F. Wright's 1971 monograph, *Arnold Bennett, Romantic Realist*[180], which would seem to be a structuralist study of romanticism in Bennett. However, it contains no functional references to Wordsworth besides a cursory mention in relation to the short story "The Death of Simon Fuge" in which the main protagonist recites a few lines by the poet. Thus, a monograph, which should have demonstrated the romantic background to the story, reveals grave limitations in this regard. It is hardly surprising, therefore, that a critic of the Edwardian period, James Hepburn expressed a very negative view of Wright's study: "Walter Wright's book will not change anything, in America or England. It is a modest book by someone who has read and liked Bennett and who wants to set down his observations"[181]. As a

---

179 J. Hillis Miller justly observes that "the literary work is self-authorizing", *op. cit.*, p.113.

180 Walter F. Wright, *Arnold Bnnett: Romantic Realist*, Lincoln, University of Nebraska Press, 1971.

181 James Hepburn, "Arnold Bennett, Romantic Realist", *Modern Philology*, 71, 2 (November 1973), p. 234. The title of Walter Wright's book is also the title of a

consequence, there still needs to be an investigation into the romantic elements of Bennett's ethical thought and, above all, his re-evaluation and contextualization of Wordsworth's poetics.

3. In light of the above considerations, it would be fruitful to consider the theme of romanticism in Bennett's novel *Accident*[182] where the cult of Wordsworth is not limited to a simple allusion or sententious quotation, but implies an active participation in the diegetic process. In fact, the plot of *Accident* is based around the contrast between advanced modern technology (here represented by a train and the European railway network in which the story develops) and the English countryside, conceived as a moral space in which the individual is liberated from the imprisonment of urbanisation and discovers the spiritual dimension that industrial society seems to have eliminated from human life. It is on the basis of this paradigmatic conflict that the figure of Alan Frith-Walter, who, in many ways, embodies many of Bennett's ideals (above all in his devotion to Wordsworth) is constructed.

However, Bennett's character is unable to observe the world with the same imaginative power with which Wordsworth created his "Poetry of Humble Life". For the decades that separate the Romantic poet from Alan Frith-Walter have altered not only the natural landscape but also Englishmen themselves who are now obsessed with the myth of success, velocity, money and the accumulation of wealth. Consequently, within the character's psychic and ontological landscape, the ideals of Romanticism are counterbalanced by the recurrent image of disaster, in the character's constant fear that everything is on the verge of collapse.

---

detailed review (pp. 233–235). At another point, the critic notes how the image of Bennett overcome with depression does not completely correspond with reality: "[...] one might even concede that Bennett was sadder, more reserved, and more anxious than most men. But he was also more vigorous, more humorous, more compassionate" (p. 234).

182 Arnold Bennett tells of a railway accident in which he was involved in France, both in a letter to H.G. Wells' wife and in a memorable page from his diary on 8 July 1911. Harris Wilson, *op.cit.,* p. 177. "[...] My train ran off the line at Mantes. First two coaches pitched over. Front part of my coach telescoped, and the whole coach smashed. For a few seconds I was in a storm of glass, flying doors, and hand-luggage. All over in ten seconds [...]".

In this sense, if modernity is a question of the thrill of velocity, Alan is an antimodern. In fact, his relationship with society is characterised by his increasing sense of dismay at the fact that England has lost its sense of pleasure in observing the natural environment without being beleaguered by the commercial terrorism of the clock. Clearly, one must only imagine the values implicit in Wordsworth's walking expeditions to realise that slowness for the Romantics entailed the possibility of relating with the natural world in which the most casual rural stroll could reserve surprising discoveries. As Adam Sisman has noted, the friendship between the two poets was made up of long excursions on foot that often lasted for weeks and which were a reflection of their love of the landscape:

> Over the next three weeks they would criss-cross the Lakes, exploring along the dales and over the passes, trekking across the fells, climbing the steep slopes, relishing the magnificent views from the peaks, and pausing to admire the many spectacular waterfalls. This being Wordsworth country, they were often able to stay the night under the roof of an acquaintance or relative[183].

In *Accident* the world characterised by leisure, friendship and solidarity is a sort of distant echo that only the protagonist can hear in the clanking trains and chaotic metropolitan world. It is no accident that, from a technological point of view, in the historical moment in which the story takes place, the train represents the symbol of a changing world that has no time to ponder the mysteries of nature. As Ian Carter has written, the train and the railway station become the epitome of modern life[184]. Another historian of means of communication, Daniel R. Headrick, also observes: "Railroads are more than trucks and trains: they are a whole new way of life, the forerunners of a new civilization"[185].

The opening sequence of the novel explicitly presents the terms of this paradigmatic opposition: the slowness of the romantic excursion

---

183 Adam Sisman, *The Friendship Wordsworth and Coleridge*, New York and London, Penguin, 2006, p. 281.

184 Ian Carter, *Railways and Culture in Britain: The Epitome of Modernity*, Manchester and New York, Manchester University Press, 2001.

185 Daniel R. Headrick, *The Tools of Empire: Technology and European Imperialism in the Nineteenth Century*, New York, Oxford University Press, 1981, p. 187.

and the speed imposed by progress. On the one hand, the commotion of the crowd in Victoria Station, on the other, the semantic universe of a text, the *Prelude*, which could be considered the quintessence of Wordsworth's aesthetics and, at the same time, a polemical reply to the industrial revolution and the damage it has inflicted on the natural landscape:

> It was a fine sharp morning, midway between Christmas and the New Year. Alan Frith-Walter drove down to Victoria in a smart, new, orange-coloured taxi. He had in his hand a slim volume, Wordsworth's *The Prelude*, at whose opening pages he had been glancing with agreeable anticipation of sustained and lofty pleasure to come. He was a business man of some culture, who, however, rarely meddled with poetry. But of late he had encountered the work of Matthew Arnold, and Arnold's solemn and convincing praise of Wordsworth had directed him to the author of *The Prelude*. He felt at once that he had not been misled. He felt that Wordsworth was his own destined poet. In the first fifty lines were a dozen phrases that flicked his imagination[186].

The significant way in which the *Prelude* is foregrounded here is particularly striking. It is almost as if Wordsworth's poem were more important than the journey to Italy that the protagonist is about to embark upon. Not only is the *Prelude* cited in detail several times in the following pages, but even in the opening sentences Wordsworth's text is inscribed in a purely literary discourse. It is also no accident that the protagonist reveals he has discovered the poem through the solemn and convincing critical judgement of Matthew Arnold. Thus, from Wordsworth, the attention seems to shift to Arnold who, as has been observed, is the most Wordsworthian of Victorian authors. As Stephen Gill says: "Arnold is the one major Victorian writer of whom it can be said without metaphor that he was nurtured in the Wordsworthian presence"[187]. In constructing his novel, Bennett shows no reserve in

---

186 Arnold Bennett, *Accident*, Kelly Bray (UK), House of Stratus, 2008, p. 1. Henceforth all quotations refer to this edition and indicated in the text as *AC* followed by page numbers.

187 Gill, *op. cit.*, p. 174. This means that during 1831–32, Matthew Arnold, who was only nine years old, had been in close contact with Wordsworth and his sister Dorothy since his father Thomas Arnold loved to spend his holidays in the Lake District, not far from where Wordsworth lived. Consequently, Arnold had the

assuming a poetic stance that, to a certain degree, suggests an alternative attitude to an aggressive and almost inhuman way of life. In spite of this, however, the character should not be associated with Wordsworth's text. Firstly, the *Prelude* is a poem that Alan Frith-Walter has only recently discovered. Secondly, as a businessman preoccupied with money, he has never considered poetry to be of any particular value to him. However, he soon realises the importance of Wordsworth's text as a means to interpret and understand the nature of life. Indeed, it is significant that he does not leave the volume in his suitcase but clasps it firmly in one hand as if it were a Bible defending him from the forces of evil.

Thus, the opening page of the novel defines the aesthetic coordinates of a character who, although he tends to look back to the past, for personal and economic reasons, is forced to observe the signs of the present in anticipation of future developments and erroneously believes that his reading of the *Prelude* will help him to solve his resulting anxieties and contradictions. In this respect, the quotation from Arnold is no coincidence. For Arnold also conveyed in his poetry the anxieties of a post-Darwinian world together with a Romantically inspired ecological-nostalgic vision of life – which is why his mentality is closer to that of the main protagonist than Wordsworth's. It must also be underlined that although he is presented as a cosmopolitan businessman who has total confidence in the resolving power of money, Alan Frith-Walter bears the traits of a cultural sensibility which make him an alter ego of the narrator.

In this respect, it is interesting to note how, during the course of the novel, the protagonist alternates between his sense of the destructive technology of the railway and his escape towards the tranquil English landscape. It is therefore significant that the *de luxe* train with which Alan, after departing from Victoria Station, intends to reach the Ligurian coast, finds itself blocked in the middle of the countryside in Kent:

> No luxury here. Nothing but the naked bones and backbone and bottom foundation of a system. .Here a train de luxe was no better than a goods-train or a

---

opportunity of listening to the poet reciting his unpublished verses to the enthusiasm of his father.

third-class excursion-train. All luxury seemed forlorn, pathetic, comic, fragile
as a bride-cake: for ever under threat of destruction. Disaster. God was not in his
heaven (*AC*, p. 17).

In his anti-Romantic rationality, Alan ponders the absurdity of finding
himself imprisoned in a *de luxe* carriage in the middle of the countryside for no apparent reason and no plausible justification other than
that of a catastrophic event. In fact, the accident is sufficient to evoke
in the protagonist's mind the vision of a disaster the effect of which he
seeks to mitigate by thinking of his favourite poet and reflecting on the
English landscape, the transformations it has undergone through industrialisation, the initial stages of trade and the sense of abandonment as
a result of his loneliness and the fact of being a stranger among many
other travellers. Alan wants to understand what has happened but, with
nobody near him, is forced to give up the attempt:

He stood on the high threshold of the car and looked at the lovely soft, bare,
variegated landscape, and the tender sky above it, and wondered for the tenth
of a second what Wordsworth would have thought about them. "Lines written
in a train halted in the midst of a Kentish landscape". Would Wordsworth have
ignored the big placard established in a meadow opposite naming the name of a
magic medicine and the number of miles from London? (*AC*, p. 16).

In his anxiety and dismay, Alan finds himself identifying with
Wordsworth to such an extent that he wonders how the poet would have
behaved in his place. He decides that Wordsworth would have found
salvation though writing. The accident would probably have triggered
in the Romantic poet a mythmaking process in which he would have
condemned the railway world, technology and industrialisation. This
process of identification does not only concern the train but also the
landscape of Kent spoiled by advertising placards and signs indicating
the distance from London. Against the anxiety of technology, Romantic aesthetics becomes, for Alan, an ethical refuge and a space in which
to find the reasons to believe and live in spite of the great transformations that have occurred in society and, above all, the perception of
imminent disaster precisely because it is associated with speed and a
world that seems to be travelling too fast to find the time to appreciate
the beauty of the universe.

Accident is a text in which almost every chapter contains either a direct or an indirect reference to Wordsworth's poetry and aesthetics. Like the beginning, the end of the novel is also marked by the poet's presence. In fact, after numerous vicissitudes on the railway and a plot that calls into question politics, society and the relationship between father and son, the main protagonist eventually reaches his wife Elaine in Italy in a sort of haven for his troubled soul that only wants to enjoy a period of Wordsworthian contemplation in tranquillity:

> "Yes", thought Alan, while Elaine sat meditative and a little tearful in her dignity. "There'll be storm. Thyphoons. But she'll stick to it. New strength required daily. I'm dashed if I don't read everything Wordsworth ever wrote, because never again shall I be without a care" (*AC*, p. 237).

In spite of his vaguely ironic and self-ironic tone, Alan concludes his silent reflection with a cultural commitment: to read every single line written by Wordsworth, For the work he has read has been a safe conduct that has helped him to overcome numerous hardships, not to mention two terrible railway accidents and the fear of his son Jack's divorce. Now he is finally on the coast of Liguria, Alan can look around and, while he observes Elaine's sadness as she bids farewell to her son who is leaving with his wife, he seems to realise that the only salvation is in Romantic poetry or rather, in this specific case, the verses of his favourite poet.

4. As has been seen, *Accident* is the story of a series of railway accidents which thematise the paradigm of ontological insecurity where visions of disaster turn an autobiographical experience into a source of literary inspiration. If Bennett's description of the railway accident in his letter of 1911 to Mrs Wells achieves the effect of immediate involvement ("I was in a storm of glass, flying doors, and hand-luggage"), the words in his journal convey a certain degree of detachment towards the same event which had occurred only the day previously:

> On Thursday I went to see the [T. B.] Wellses at Pont de l'Arche. I came back yesterday, and found myself in a railway accident at Mantes. 6 wounded.
>   [...] I was in a sort of large Pullmanesque compartment at the back of a first-class coach, two or three coaches from the engine. The windows broke. The corridor door sailed into the compartment. My stick flew out of the rack. The table smashed itself. I clung hard to the arms of my seat, and fell against an

armchair in front of me. There was a noise of splintering, and there were various other noises. An old woman lay on the floor crying. I wondered: "Shall I remain unharmed until the thing stops?" Immense tension of waiting for the final stoppage. Equilibrium at last and I was unhurt[188].

Here the description is some pages longer and marked by a precision of detail which reveals the talent of a writer more than an intention on the part of someone to record their memories in a diary. In fact, the journal contains details that already suggest the outlines of a story:

I remember the face of one wounded woman was all over coal and dust. We had shaved a short goods train standing on the next line, and the tender of the train was against our coach. A young American said that it was sticking into our coach, but I don't think it was. He said that the front part of our coach was entirely telescoped, but it wasn't entirely telescoped. It was, however, all smashed up. My impression is of a total wreck brought about in a few seconds[189].

It is no accident that Bennett concludes the entry in his diary with the following words: "I really was upset under my superficial calmness"[190]. Although the railway accident caused no injuries and left no particular signs of psychological trauma, it would leave a profound mark on the writer's literary sensibility. Several years later, his memories of the experience would inspire the novel *Accident* (1929), which Bennett wrote from the end of 1926 until July 1927. Exactly fifteen years later, his imagination transformed the dramatic event in Mantes into a metaphor of the human condition: life is constantly uncertain and individuals have little control over the course of their destinies. As Walter F. Wright, has rightly observed, in *Accident* Bennett dramatizes a view of life which had already taken root in his personal view of life: "Long before he wrote the story *Accident* Bennett was intrigued with the fact that an unexpected event of hardly a moment's duration could demolish a man's world, render meaningless whatever philosophy he had constructed, and destroy the very personality which he had struggled to maintain"[191]. This is precisely the kind of transformation

---

188   Bennett, *The Journals*, cit., p. 342.
189   *Ibid.,* p. 343.
190   *Ibidem.*
191   Wright, *op.cit.*, p. 168.

that is highlighted in the novel which, unlike the Victorian period, is linked with a way of life based on velocity and the new means of transport[192]. In Bennett's stories, trains are no longer the locomotives described by Dickens. With the development of technology and increasing safety and, comfort (luxurious compartments, restaurant carriages etc) the train has become a means with which to travel from Calais to Paris and from Paris to Italy in only a few hours. In light of such progress, railway accidents become more traumatic and disturbing for the passengers involved.

Thus, the idea of velocity is linked to that of a catastrophe which may occur in a few seconds and cause a dramatic impact on individual lives. This notion had always fascinated Bennett who saw human life as an unresolvable enigma. In his view, there is something incomprehensible about a cosmic order that is able to deprive human beings of their dignity and self-respect. In the central chapter of the novel, Bennett summarises this view in a few lines in which he comments on the railway accident by revealing man's finitude and weakness before the events that overcome him and reduce him to an inferior animal:

> Only a few seconds earlier he had been secure, proud, assessing the far future without any sense of the ridiculousness of so doing. Now the future was brutally, implacably, lopped to the limit of another few seconds, and he had been diminished to a helpless insect under the indifferent heel of fate. He felt sick, without manhood, without dignity or self-respect. He would have sold his soul to be out of the murderous train, in a field, anywhere far from the line (*AC*, p. 129).

The novel is permeated with images of disaster where the anxieties of the real author seem to converge with the thought of what the "railway accident at Mantes" could have been like in terms of loss of human lives, including his own. In fact, it is precisely this potentially tragic and

---

192 On the significance of the train in terms of the theme of modernity, see Ian Carter, *op. cit.* With regard to the English novel, the critic devotes a whole chapter to *Dombey and Sons* (1846–48) which, as is known, describes a railway accident in which Dickens himself was involved. Carter also briefly analyses *Accident*, which he places in the tradition of the English social novel: "This is a 'condition of England' novel, written eighty years after Dickens, Disraeli and Elizabeth Gaskell" (p. 152). Obviously, this association seems totally inappropriate in that *Accident* contains none of the social conflicts we find in the authors cited.

catastrophic event which triggers a series of reflections around which Bennett widens the diegetic scope of the narration to insert another, profoundly personal story which, from the point of view of the narrative structure, constitutes the backbone of *Accident*, and determines its development and conclusion. The story inserted concerns the *romance* which has often led critics to accuse Bennett of sentimentalism. However, in this case, it would be appropriate to recall that, as early as 1920, Sidney Hayes Cox would come to Bennett's defence regarding his romantic interpretation of the real events of his story: "The obvious romantic vitality displayed in Mr. Bennett's versatile and crowded career may be a slight evidence of the perception of romance in life"[193]. As shall be seen, in *Accident*, the writer foregrounds the element of *romance* as the locus in which he grounds his idea of disaster as an inevitable aspect of the human condition.

5. If the novel is considered from the point of view of the perception and interpretation of reality, it must be immediately stated that the main protagonist, Alan Frith-Walter, is a keenly sensitive, mature man who is able to detect every kind of psychological nuance. Yet, in spite of the fact that Frith-Walter is presented to the reader as an artist with an ability to see to the heart of things, in reality he is a representative of the privileged classes of Great Britain with no economic problems of any kind and a well-known surname[194]. The image conveyed to the reader in the first description of Alan is of a man who has everything to be self-confident about and not one who, on the contrary, will find himself at the mercy of a series of uncertain events that transform his life into an inaccessible journey: "He had been born well, adored by very sensible parents, well educated in a modern manner under the direction of a wise father. He had succeeded to an ample share in a vast manufacturing business. He had married satisfactorily. Nothing in his wife of the spoilt, faded beauty making hell around her by antics of over-indulged nerves!" (*AC*, p. 12). Alan Frith-Walter has all the characteristics of a man of success who, at the same time, is fortunate enough to have had everything from life that he could possibly desire. Given

---

193   Cox, *op. cit.*, p. 359.

194   The protagonist's double-barrelled name is a clear indication of his social position and Bennett is clearly aware that his reader will make such an association.

these socio-economic assumptions and the elitist context in which luxury, privilege and opulence abound, we can only imagine the portrait of Alan Frith-Walter as that of a middle-aged man who spends his time visiting Italy and travelling to the most important capital cities of Europe, always followed by his faithful secretary, appropriately named Miss Office, whose business is to relieve her master of all the tasks that concern the organisation of his journeys and his relations with others.

From a socio-economic angle, Alan Frith-Walter is the embodiment of success with an only son, John, affectionately called Jack, to guarantee the continuity of the family lineage and its immense patrimony, who will not need to face the problem of sharing his inheritance with others. His portrait is marked by a sense of euphoria from a psychological point of view, since destiny has been very kind to Alan Frith-Walter. However, beneath the visible surface that confirms this interpretation of the protagonist's biography lies what others fail to see; the perception of reality which, precisely because it is deeply-rooted, ignores social conditions and material comforts and does not know the danger of an improvidence or a financial crash. On the other hand, it is possible to be wealthy and inwardly fragile. In Alan's case, his relationship with reality is conditioned by the image of the disaster. From the position of his social and economic privilege, the protagonist believes he can detect disaster around the corner. It is with this sense of terror which pertains to the visible dimension that he travels through Europe doing his best to give a meaning to his life and somehow try to dodge the psychological process which seems to undermine his relations with others and his own *Weltanschauung*.

Alan Frith-Walter's anxiety is apparent from the opening of the novel as he prepares for his journey to the continent to reach his wife on the Ligurian coast. While making his way to Victoria Station by taxi, he begins to read some lines from Wordsworth's *Prelude* which seem to describe his own emotional state while seeking a sensation of freedom that only escape from the city can offer him.[195] As noted previously, poetry is not able to distract him from the threat of an

---

195 It would be worthwhile to quote some of the lines from Book I of Wordsworth's Prelude which appear in the opening sequence of *Accident*: "[...] escaped/From the vast city, where I long had pined" (vv. 6–7); "The earth is all before me" (v. 14); "Dear Liberty!" (v. 31); "[...] the sweet breath of heaven/ Was blowing on my body, felt within/A correspondent breeze, that gently moved/ With quickening

imminent disaster with catastrophic consequences. In fact, once he is in the station and unable to find his secretary, he already begins to imagine that Miss Office has been involved in a car accident: "She might be injured. The luggage might be spread abroad on some roadway, and Miss Office being driven unconscious to a hospital. Frightful complications. He would miss the train. In which case he would miss the boat. In which case he would miss the continental train. In which case he would miss the rendezvous with his wife" (*AC*, p. 2). In spite of the groundless nature of these these pessimistic conjectures, like many others in the text, the narrative is pervaded by a sense of perpetual anxiety. Alan tries to banish his anxiety by studying the various types of people with whom he comes into contact. Thus, the expression of the taxi driver who reinforces Alan's faith in decency and common sense. Even his secretary is placed in the category of positive people, being an honest and determined woman capable of dominating "the potentialities of emotion" (*AC*, p. 8). In this respect, Victoria Station becomes a locus of separation, a space in movement in contrast, for example, with the immobility of an official ("fixed and stable", *AC*, p. 6) and other representatives of more modest social classes such as the porters, the drivers and a lubricator which the luxury train very soon leaves behind. The sense of the contrast is always uppermost in Alan's thoughts, all the more so in the light of Wordsworth's poem which he particularly admires for the attention it devotes to common people:

> "Why are we going, and why are they helping us to go?" thought Alan. "And why do they not storm the trains and take our place by force? All have their cares, and *I have not a care in the world*. These contrasts on the platform at Victoria are really too spectacular... How crudely I am thinking! Still, *I have not a care in the world*. But the world is my care". He fingered the volume of Wordsworth in the pocket of his new blue overcoat (*AC*, pp. 7–8, my italics).

The repetition of the phrase "I have not a care in the world" suggests the protagonist's awareness of his privileged position but also his feelings of guilt. For he realizes that opulence and prosperity are possible only

---

virtue" (vv. 33–36); "a cheerful confidence in things to come" (v. 58) in William Wordsworth, *The Prelude*, Harmondsworth, Penguin, 1971.

through the exploitation of those less fortunate who do not even seem conscious of their condition of inferiority.

The point of view of Alan – a fifty-year-old man who, in an excess of self-criticism, admits he has learnt everything except how to live – becomes even more critical when he observes the wealthy travellers who, equally unaware, seem to be fleeing from their own lives: "What a cargo of fleshly ideals and aspirings!" (*AC*, p. 10). However, it is obvious that these travellers are void of spiritual ideals. What animates the *de luxe* carriage departing for Paris is not the internal world which Alan detects in Wordsworth's verses but the materialistic spirit of the flesh and money. Nevertheless, once they arrive at Boulogne Station, all contrasts are annulled as the passengers move about at the customs like a mass of disorientated sheep with piles of luggage containing their most intimate secrets. From his dysphoric perspective, Alan imagines a society in which the station represents a form of social encounter that leads directly to the negation of the individual personality:

> [...] there were no rich and no poor and no gentlemen and no ladies; none but sheep vitalised by fear, impatience and resentment. Civilization was destroyed, and men lived as though it had never been, shameless under the gaze of blue-smocked porters who were not men but numbered myrmidons of some mysterious far-off deity omnipotent and terrible (*AC*, p. 24).

It is easy to detect the weakness that presides over Alan's interpretation of reality. For, after having exalted in the magnificent verses of his favourite poet, rather than accept the fact that life is made up of good days and bad, exciting and depressing events, passion and delusion – he seems to reach a breaking point merely as a result of the chaos in Boulogne Station which he simplistically interprets as the end of civilization At the same time, the protagonist reveals once again a pessimism that contrasts strikingly with the optimism of his prestigious social position. Beneath this pessimistic vision lies an interpretation of life as a series of disasters which, essentially, is what constitutes the main theme of the novel.

6. On the surface, the images of disaster that haunt Alan concern railway accidents and their powerful effect on the general public, particularly through sensationalistic newspaper reports. Actually, from the very moment he climbs on board the *de luxe* carriage bound for Paris

and Genoa through the Moncenisio tunnel, the protagonist begins to imagine a potentially disastrous railway accident. Yet this level of the diegesis conceals another more private and less visible level from a social viewpoint that concerns the disasters which loom over personal relationships and, what is particularly distressing for a Victorian gentleman, those of his family. It is no accident that Alan is travelling to the Ligurian coast anxious to join his wife at Arenzano, where he hopes to spend his time in tranquillity contemplating the beauty of the Mediterranean. As already mentioned, the real disaster does not concern the purely public dimension of the story so much as the private sphere which very soon convinces Alan that nothing can be considered safe from catastrophe.

Alan's mind, where every action is systematically and scrupulously planned, becomes troubled by a destabilising factor that concerns his personal life when he believes he sees his daughter-in-law, Pearl, known in the English *beau monde* as Mrs John Frith-Walter, aboard the same train he is about to catch. Initially, the protagonist refuses to believe what he has seen and even questions the visible sphere upon which he bases most of his sensations. However, the very idea that Pearl could be on the train bound for the continent puts him into a state of agitation which culminates in his perception of a private menace. Like the Frith-Walters, Pearl's family is among the wealthiest of the United Kingdom and, consequently, the girl's social behaviour is the same as her husband Jack's characterised by freedom of movement as the expression of ideological freedom. As the reader learns later, Pearl's mother spends her winters in Viareggio where she feels very much at home thanks to the large presence of an English community in Tuscany.

From Alan's point of view, the possibility that he has made a mistake is his sole hope against the abyss that has opened up in his imagination in which he already sees in that girl alone on the train the signs of a matrimonial disaster. Haunted by the spectre of a catastrophe, Alan sees Pearl as a positive force, since he has always admired the girl for her beauty and progressive way of thinking. Once at the customs in Boulogne, when Alan is certain that the girl he has seen is indeed Pearl, he is overcome by a sense of impending disaster:

It was just as they were leaving the Custom House, under the inimical gaze of two sentinel soldiers, that Alan for no reason whatever turned his head to glance at the thinning throng behind, and saw Pearl – unmistakably. Instantly he felt the weight anew on his heart. Her face recalled his son's wedding. He saw her again exactly as he had seen her in the motorcar, with Jack looking rather an abashed simpleton by her side, driving away to the station for the honeymoon. A face composed and somehow commanding, the face of one fully equal to the situation. A lovely blonde, with a perfect complexion [...].

He was afraid. Why had there been no word from Pearl, no word from Jack? Of course the girl had not the least idea that her father-in-law would be tra- velling by just that Continental service; for neither he nor Jack was an ardent letter-writer, and he knew that mother-in-law and daughter-in-law rarely corres- ponded. Why had the girl left England? Where was she going? It struck him that her mother, an enigmatic creature whom Pearl apparently adored, might already be in the South, in one of those fashionable hotels in which she passed her life, and that her daughter was joining her. But why? The mother might be ill. No! The mother had a constitution of leather and was never ill. No! A married daugh- ter in conjugal difficulties flew to an adored mother for moral support. That must be, was, the solution of the puzzle (*AC*, pp. 27–28).

In the increasing succession of questions and negative hypotheses, we may recognise the psychological traits of the protagonist who, in the context of a society in rapid transformation, is only able to inter- pret reality in destructive and self-destructive terms. For undoubtedly, Pearl's visit represents a fracture in a well organised scheme which would see the world as a place void of problems. Against change, Alan opposes a maniacal search for social and moral order and it is precisely this desire for practical and psychic stability that determines a state of permanent instability which, after confirmation of Pearl's presence on the train, culminates in his endless anxiety. The questions he poses are the reflection of such an anxiety that shifts the ontological empha- sis from the external space (the railway accident with its consequent deaths and devastation) to an internal space the desolate landscapes of which are no longer public but private. It is not a simple affirmation of uncertainty or precariousness: Pearl's entrance on the scene brings the warning signs of conjugal disaster which, in the protagonist's selfish view, is the most terrible thing that could enter his private sphere. The- refore, he sees in the potential marital failure of his son, his own failure and, as a result, is overcome by a painful uncertainty.

It comes as no surprise when, even after greeting Pearl and inquiring her about her journey, Alan continues with his self-questioning, almost as if he is trying to evade the truth which he has, more or less consciously, already perceived from the tone of his daughter-in-law's replies:

> He was suddenly drawn towards Pearl; he had the charming sensation of genuine intimacy with the exquisite strong creature. Strange! For he also went in fear of her. Beyond question Jack had chosen something worth choosing. But was Jack – a fine fellow in many ways – worthy of the choice he had made? A pretty doubt for a father! However, in these moments Alan was not a father, nor a father-in-law. He was just Pearl's appreciative fellow-creature, and beginning to luxuriate in her society, in his discovery of her individuality (*AC*, p. 53).

Attracted by Pearl's beauty, Alan initially delays the moment of revealing himself and postpones further investigation in favour of a gratifying complacency that derives from the mere presence of his daughter-in-law whom he regards as a model of intelligence, beauty and sensitivity. With his discovery of the girl's temperament, at least on a superficial level, Alan feels they are both on the same side and is proud to note the striking contrast between her open-mindedness and the narrow-mindedness and backwardness of the other women. With her strength of character and determination and absence of prejudice or obscurantist superstitions, Pear appears as the epitome of the New Woman: "Yes, he liked her style. No nerves, no superstition, no nonsense about her [...] A man could have peace with her, in the full assurance that she would not outrage his masculine commonsense" (*AC*, p. 54). Significantly, the narrative focus is placed on the man's reactions to Pearl's beauty, maturity and self-confidence: "How sharp she was! And how agreeable her phrasing! How worldly! Worldliness, he decided, was the quality which best appealed to him" (*AC*, p. 55). Ironically, Pearl's rehabilitation in Alan's eyes is expressed in worldly terms as opposed to the spiritual values professed in Wordsworth's work which he had upheld and admired so much at the start of his journey.

In reality, although the protagonist projects himself as a straightforward and coherent person, he is far from firm in his judgments. Indeed, in both his internal monologues and conversations with others, Alan is a man who always wavers between positive and negative poles.

Thus, after spending some time with her and behaving almost as if he were not her father-in-law, Alan's positive assessment of Pearl is soon transformed into a negative judgment when she reveals that she is effectively fleeing from her husband for reasons connected with his political vocation. Thus, behind her escape there is no betrayal, ambiguity or moral corruption. Jack has simply decided to engage in politics because he no longer wants to spend his life like his father, travelling from one train to the next in the continual search for something to heal him from his restlessness, anxiety and profound pessimism. Jack's nature is very different from his father's because his political passion is an authentic vocation and his wife, who would rather see him conform to the Victorian ideal of a husband and defend his own privileges rather than concern himself with the unfortunate in society, is rebelling precisely against this authenticity.

7. In the second part of *Accident* it becomes clear that the clash involves above all the contrast between the public and private sphere. In fact, although he is directly involved in a railway disaster, Alan only recognises his own private disaster. The possibility that his son's marriage may fail at any moment is for him the most painful expression of disaster. Thus, when he witnesses the discussions between his son and Pearl, the protagonist immediately sums up: "They were implacably divided, those two savages. Alan saw clearly in their demeanour *the seed of the disaster, inevitable, which he had feared and which would for ever shame the family*" (*AC*, p. 157, my italics). The symbolic tension with which the railway journey is invested almost becomes irrelevant in comparison with his personal catastrophe. John Lucas has rightly identified this transition to the detriment of the broader social theme of the novel:

> The catastrophe turns out to be in no way symbolic of the train of fools over which Alan's conscience has been so active. Indeed, all the larger issues and questions are lost sight of in the second half of the novel. We are asked to consider that the crucial question is whether Pearl will return to Jack. The whole book does an abrupt about-turn. What had been a novel dealing allusively but powerfully with contemporary society now becomes a novel operating on a purely domestic level[196].

---

196   Lucas, *op. cit.*, p. 218.

Lucas's analysis is very pertinent. However, it must be said that the public and private spheres are directly linked by Jack's decision which triggers Pearl's negative response as she decides to abandon him the moment he informs her that, as a man committed to social justice, he has decided to stand as a candidate for the Labour Party at the forthcoming elections. It is no accident that in Alan's reaction private and public interests clash. For in learning of his son's decision, his attitude becomes more ambivalent since he is convinced that "his son's simplicity and sincerity and directness" (*AC*, p. 188) is the result of his fundamental honesty of which, as his father, he can only be proud. This notion is counteracted by the need to attend to the interests of the family which, as Alan knows very well, cannot be pursued by becoming a member of Parliament for the Labour Party: "And here was the boy creating an enormous mess in the family and about to create a still more enormous mess in a stable and conservative country! The prospect of the future was worse than disquieting; it was terrifying" (*AC*, p. 188). His daughter-in-law moves along the same lines as she also assumes that the absolute prerogative of his life should be the safeguarding of his family:

> "[…] He's pretending to himself there isn't a class war already. But there is a class war. And there always was and there always will be. As if all politics weren't class war! And if there isn't a class war, who's going to begin one? Not us. It's Labour that's out for a class war. Not that I care so much about class. What I care about is my family, and yours too. When you really get down to bedrock, the family's the most important thing" (*AC*, p. 195).

Jack becomes isolated as a result of the family's disapproval of his decision. In this case, *family* is a term designed to conceal something else: the terror of the Frith-Walters of losing all their social privileges. Alan, who has no doubt of this, knows that his son's political vocation will have to deal with the interests of the world in which the young man has been formed. Thus, Alan and Pearl find themselves on common ground in their defence of their social class:
The family for him was more sacred than anything else in the social structure. It was the main article of his religion. And, though she had slighted marriage to him, how she had defended the family! She cared tremendously for the ornaments of existence; she was without doubt

luxurious. But her preoccupation with powder and rouge, the cut of frocks, manners, the arts of elegance, did not prevent her from having basic ideas about life (*AC*, p. 195).

In the world of the wealthy there can be no other vocation besides the defence of one's wealth. In this sense, Jack's political vocation is the real catastrophe which, when associated with the potential failure of his marriage, evokes the most sombre visions in Alan's mind. Nevertheless, it must also be said that after reaching its public and private climax (the railway accident and Pearl's escape from her husband), the story finds an unexpected resolution in Italy when all the protagonists, still immersed in their unresolved conflicts, meet on the Ligurian coast. Jack, who is also a part of this group because of the risk of his final separation from Pearl, is accompanied by a friend on a plane from France in pursuit of his wife. The novel being set in the 1920s, there clearly seems to be no problem for the populist rebel Jack, to reach his wife on board a private airplane. Pearl is also struck by the sensational nature of this action which she sees as a testimony of his love. However, Jack's venture is insufficient in atoning the girl's hostility as she still holds on to the idea that a husband who is a member of the Labour Party will only bring her disgrace for the rest of her life. Harassed by his parents, Jack fails to overcome his internal conflicts by giving the upper hand to his political vocation and, after a sleepless night, he abandons the idea of a political career in the Labour Party, a fierce and antitraditional political formation in which neither the Frith-Walters nor Pearl recognise themselves. Thus arrives the turning point of the story where Pearl, who learns that Jack is willing to bury his political ambitions in order not to lose her love, realises that she has won the battle. Her punctilious determination disappears and, to the great surprise of Jack's parents, she tells him it would be wrong to suffocate his vocation:

> "[...] All I say is you aren't going to give up any career for me. And I shan't leave you. If you must ruin your native country, I'll stand in with you. What does it matter? All politics are silly. No, they aren't. Well, I don't know what I mean" (*AC*, p. 235).

Although her ideological confusion remains, Pearl nevertheless takes a decision regarding Jack's political venture and promises she will stay by his side regardless. Thus, after being represented as a model New

Woman, Pearl is made to withdraw into the ranks of the traditional Victorian female where a woman must be psychologically dependent on her man whatever the consequences. The private disaster evoked and almost encountered many times does not occur. The happy ending marks the individual itinerary of the protagonist who can only conclude that if seen from afar: "Disaster might be splendid". In fact, as the family conflicts are resolved and the matrimonial crisis of his son is avoided, Alan Frith-Walter can simply engross himself in the sensation of reassuring beauty and feel like one who, taking a backward glance, sees the end of any idea of disaster[197]. Thus, the universal order, which is so important to Alan, is re-established while the problems of the British working-class, at least for the moment, may be put to one side in anticipation of the future success of Jack the "Bolshevik"[198]

---

197 In a similar way to the Victorian novel, Bennett's story shows, as occurs in the positive epilogue to *Accident*, his tendency to untie the knots by placing an emphasis on human understanding and the capacity of men to finally find a common language. This is precisely what happens with Jack and Pearl.

198 Here, incidentally, it must be noted that when Jack's mother, Elaine, learns of the conversion of her son to the Labour Party, she does not hesitate to blame her daughter-in-law for using his political vocation as an excuse to leave her husband: "I'm so disappointed in Pearl that I can't say how disappointed I am! Why, if your father had turned Bolshevik do you imagine I should have cut loose from him? A wife! Why, even if he had committed murder – surely wives have a duty" (pp. 220–221). Elaine clearly represents the model of a woman extremely hostile to the world of the New Woman and the suffragettes, in line with a more Victorian reactionary tradition.

CONCLUSION

If we consider Bennett's fiction from a socio-historical angle, we can say that the Potteries are represented by the writer in all their complexity while granting nothing to nostalgia and romanticism. As Margaret Drabble has written, there is always a provincial dimension in Bennett which is part of his way of perceiving the contrast between the rich and the poor: "[...] he could not disguise the fact that for him the luxury hotel was something of a private obsession, deeply rooted in his own provincialism, his own early deprivations, his own claustrophobia in the cloying domestic scene"[199]. On the other hand, it is this provincialism that characterises so many of his protagonists who never forget they have behind them a primitive methodism, a wealthy middle-class and a culture that never spreads beyond its limited horizons, such as a culture of the *Grand Tour*. However, when he published one of his most interesting works, *Riceyman Steps*, in 1923, the writer proved he was able to produce stories which, in the wake of the great realist novels, were original in form and content even if they did not programmatically cater to the tastes of the general public: "[Ryceyman Steps] has that extraordinary grainy feel for place and detail which is the hallmark of Bennett's best work. The area round Kings Cross Road, with its frowsty shops, tenement buildings and dingy pubs like the Percy selling imaginably awful beer – it is as palpably there as the Bursley of earlier work"[200].

From the point of view of his literary productions, therefore, Bennett was undeniably as prolific a writer as Trollope. Both adored success and both knew how to flatter their readers. Another feature that links the two authors is the idea of a literary topology. As Trollope imagined Barsetshire, Bennett created the Five Towns. However, although Trollop's themes and motifs are totally different to those of Bennett,

---

199 Drabble, *op. cit.*, p. 342.
200 Lucas, *op. cit.*, p. 195.

Trollop also – as Hillis Miller notes – was keen on observing change in terms of conflict and social tension: "I find Anthony Trollope's novels consistently enchanting, both in their recreation of Victorian middle-class ideology and in their implicit critique of that ideology"[201]. Not only, but both Trollop and Bennett are part of the rank of writers which academia, until a few decades ago, did not deem worthy of great consideration, in that their popularity was associated with the idea of moral levity if not total evasion from society and its problems. Thus, Simon Heffer, sees Trollop and Bennett united by the same fate of critical disparagement:

> When I was reading English at university 30 years ago, Trollope was simply not considered serious. This did not necessarily count against him. Cambridge in the late 1970s and early 1980s had some funny ideas about literature. To some writers it should have been a badge of honour to be denigrated, marginalised and reviled by the panjandrums of the English faculty. I recall the contempt in which Arnold Bennett, John Galsworthy and H. G. Wells were held – for no better reason, it seemed, than that they had not been Virginia Woolf or D. H. Lawrence[202].

As a result of their popularity, Trollope and Bennett have been disregarded by critics as diverse as F. R. Leavis and Raymond Williams[203]. From a genealogical point of view, Bennett's works deliberately fuse various traditions of the Victorian novel drawing above all on Nineteenth-century novelists such as Balzac, Maupassant, Stendhal and Zola who, in spite of their different approaches to fiction, exerted an important influence on the English writer. From another angle, Bennett understood that the realist novels of George Eliot and Charles Dickens,

---

201 Miller, *op. cit.*, p. 121.
202 Simon Heffer, "Sadly, the snobs were right about Trollope", *The Telegraph*, 1 January 2011. http://www.telegraph.co.uk/comment/columnists/simonhef fer/8234543/Sadly-the-snobs-were-right-about-Trollope.html [accesso 21 settembre 2016]
203 It seems somewhat strange that in his *Culture and Society* – first published in 1958 – Raymond Williams, never mentions Arnold Bennett, in spite of the fact that Bennett's themes fall fully within the framework of the culturological topics placed under scrutiny by the noted scholar. This omission is all the more surprising when it is recalled that Williams places social and industrial change at the centre of his study. See Raymond Williams, *Culture and Society 1780–1950*, Harmondsworth, Penguin, 1971.

for example, were no longer valid representations of real life. This explains his peculiar position as a writer who is partly associated with the first wave of Modernism. In fact, the works he wrote which were least influenced by Naturalism, led him to pursue new directions in both the novel and the short story. From an anti-Victorian perspective, Bennett's novels look forward to the twentieth century with a series of innovations which were partly perceived by Henry James in a review of *The Old Wives' Tale*:

> The canvas is covered, ever so closely and vividly covered, by the exhibition of innumerable small facts and aspects, at which we assist with the most comfortable sense of their substantial truth. The sisters, and more particularly the less adventurous, are at home in their author's mind, they sit and move at their ease in the square chamber of his attention, to a degree beyond which the production of that ideal harmony between creature and creator could scarcely go, and all by an art of demonstration so familiar and so "quiet" that the truth and the poetry, to use Goethe's distinction, melt utterly together and we see no difference between the subject of the show and the showman's feeling, let alone the showman's manner, about it[204].

However, as has been demonstrated in the chapter dedicated to *The Old Wives' Tale*, the tecniques of realism perceived in Bennett's novel do not exactly correspond to James's analysis. Unlike Bennett, James wanted his reader to be completely taken aback by narrative events. In his review he deliberately stretches his critical discourse to reproach the writer of the Five Towns for fusing truth with poetry, thus giving his readers an explicit, ready-made meaning without demanding from them any effort in interpreting the text or engaging them in a reading of refined events in which they are capable of seeing the metaphors beneath the description of a face, an object, a domestic scene or a landscape. Commenting on James's prejudice against Bennett, Linda R. Anderson is correct when she observes that:

> Bennett defined art as being less important than the perception of cause and effect in nature; by doing so he also testified to the exteranality of his view of

---

204 The review is in *Henry James and W. H. Wells: A Record of Their Friendship, Their Debate on the Art of Fiction, and Their Quarrel*, ed. Leon Edel and Gordon N. Ray, Urbana, IL, and London, University of Illinois Press, 1958, p. 187.

art, the limitations of its role, as he saw it, to transform and construct reality. Bennett does not endow narrative with the power to shape events to give them more significance than they contain in themselves. For Bennett, the implications of alienation, threat and powerlessness contained in such a view could be held in check by reference to a larger sense of determinacy which could endow the bewildering and meaningless events of existence with purpose. The individual, though unable to transcend reality, is made to reconcile himself to the necessity of things, the past, what has already been defined[205].

For Anderson, it is not determinism that governs individual lives but causality. For example, in the case of *The Old Wives's Tale*, Sophia's decision to escape with Gerald Scales to Paris is an effect the cause of which is to be seen in the romantic and restless nature of the protagonist herself. As discussed above, in the third chapter her rebellious temperament causes a rift with her family and sets her in opposition with her sister Constance. On another level, the passiveness that characterises Anna Tellwright's words and actions is a consequence of her Methodist upbringing. It is because her life is determined by Methodism that she completely submits to her father's psychological tyranny which she never questions.

In a worldview based on causality, Bennett notes that there still exists a design beyond the relationship between cause and effect which always invests human destinies with new motives and tensions. Granted that Bennett never talks in terms of a *telos* and does not intend to refer to a teleological design but rather an order/disorder dialectic that eventually culminates in the recovery of an equilibrium that, even though not morally marked, assigns everything to its proper place. This is precisely what happens in works like *The Old Wives' Tale* and the Clayhanger Trilogy[206] where, as Lucas observes, "he ceases to write about the Five Towns. For Bennett is too sensitive, intelligent and perceptive a writer not to know that he can continue to study Five Towns life realistically only if he is prepared *not* to keep apart. Really keeping apart means turning to less interesting fiction"[207]. Undoubtedly, Bennett

---

205 Anderson, *op. cit.*, p. 94.
206 The trilogy consists of three novels in which the predominant setting is the Potteries: *Clayhanger* (1910), *Hilda Lessways* (1911) and *These Twain* (1916). Bennett also wrote a fourth novel, *The Roll-Call* (1918), which is only indirectly related to the project since it is set in London.
207 Lucas, *op. cit.*, p. 165.

is at his most authentic when he is dealing with the place of his origins – once he is away from the Potteries he becomes less authentic and his imagination less inspired. The very idea of realism, in its various interpretations, acquires more importance and a depth of authenticity that gives – as in the case of *The Old Wives' Tale* – a narrative tension that goes beyond the principles of realism itself, where Bennett creates what he himself called a "passionate intensity of vision"[208]. In fact, with respect to his readers he has a fundamental conviction that: "Every fine emotion produced in the reader has been, and must have been previously felt by the writer, but in a far greater degree"[209]. Behind such a statement there is obviously a certain persistence of the romantic myth of the artist which, as we have seen, the writer borrows above all from the theories of Wordsworth whose poetical works always remained an essential reference point for Bennett. According to H.G. Wells, there was something naive, something romantically innocent about Bennett's approach to reality:

> Bennett was taking the thing that is, for what it was, with a naïve and eager zest. He saw it brighter than it was; he did not see into it and did not see beyond it. He was like a child at a fair. His only trouble was how to get everything in in the time at his disposal, music, pictures, books, shows, eating, drinking, display, the remarkable clothes one could wear, the remarkable stunts one could do, the unexpected persons, the incessant fresh oddities of people; the whole adorable, incessant, multitudinous lark of it[210].

Of course, this portrait of Bennett as a writer concerned solely with 'appropriating' everything ("how to get everything in") is somewhat biased. Wells is judging the writer of the Potteries from a personal point of view rather than as a scholar of fiction. However, the idea that Bennett faces reality with a romantic spirit, only tempered in part by his self-discipline, remains true. As Wright has justly observed: "Wells was interested in remoulding the world; Bennett was much more preoccupied with self-discipline. [...] This meant building some kind of ideal concept of oneself and establishing its dominance

---

208 Bennett, *The Author's Craft*, cit., p. 45.
209 *Ibid.*
210 H. G. Wells, *Experiment in Autobiography*, New York, Macmillan, 1934, p. 535.

over recalcitrant circumstance"[211]. And even in this idea of absolute self-control, the writer declares that he is indebted to his homeland, to the world from which he came and which forged his temperament: "A proud self-unconscious self-esteem: that is what few people have. If at times it deserts me and mine, it always returns the stronger for having retreated. We are of the North, outwardly brusque, stoical, undemonstrative, scornful of the impulsive; inwardly all sentiment and crushed tenderness. We are of the North, incredibly, ruthlessly independent; and eager to say 'Damn you' to all the deities at the least hint of condescension"[212]. Again, in conclusion, the centrality of the Potteries reemerges, as, with the passing decades, they gradually move away from his metropolitan life. However, this process of estrangement, which transforms the Five Towns into a place of the memory, results in the writer mythologizing the place of his origin. It is well known that the people of the Potteries did not appreciate his representations of their daily life, their work and the Methodist congregation. The reaction of the press in that district was never favorable since many saw his novels as expressing criticism – if not contempt – for his people. Obviously, this was not the case; Bennett wanted to portray his experiences of the Five Towns realistically, while always avoiding to soften its harsh contours or tone down its moral and religious angularities, or render the tensions that existed among those who were, almost by divine decree, doomed to failure, less obvious. On the other hand, it must also be said that the industrial world from which he came had provided him with the most authentic themes for his fiction and, as he writes in the last book of The Old Wives' Tale, had taught him "What life is."

As seen in the analysis of *Accident*, Bennett was also able to handle with great skill and mastery works that took on an international perspective by thematizing tensions and conflicts that, on closer inspection, were no longer the same as those dedicated to the Five Towns. In my opinion, *The Old Wives' Tale* remains Bennett's masterpiece, both in terms of its formal organization and content. On several occasions, I have emphasized the importance of literary geography in Bennett's fiction. In his masterpiece, however, topological organization-though

---

211 Wright, *op. cit.*, p. 21.
212 Bennett, *The Journals*, cit., p. 27. (diary entry 9 December 1896).

rigorous in detail and development-gives way to an idea of temporality conceived as an objective fact against which no barrier can be raised. And it is undeniable that no other Bennett novel shows with the same imaginative power or poetic tension as *The Old Wives' Tale* the passage of time dramatized as an inner and outer transformation as well as a socio-historical transition from one era to another and from one way of living and thinking to another.

From the perspective of cultural systems, *The Old Wives' Tale* sheds light on the epistemic framework in a way few works of the same period do. Ultimately, it is in this novel that Bennett demonstrates the vitality of the world of the Potteries by evoking, in all its complexity and socioeconomic and cultural nuances, the transition through the different periods of the lives of the two protagonists, Constance and Sophia Baines. At the same time, it must be said that, beyond the characters and the geography itself, Bennett offers readers a particularly effective portrayal of the human condition and, I might add, of human weakness in the face of time which devours all things.

BIBLIOGRAPHY

Agosti, Stefano, *Enunciazione e racconto: per una semiologia della voce narrativa*, Bologna, il Mulino, 1989.

Allen, Walter, *The English Novel*, Harmondsworth, Penguin, 1984 [1954].

Ambrosini, Richard, *R. L. Stevenson: la poetica del romanzo*, Roma, Bulzoni, 2001.

Anderson, Linda R., *Bennett, Wells and Conrad: Narrative in Transition*, New York, St Martin's Press, 1988.

Barthes, Roland, *S/Z*, traduzione di Lidia Lonzi, Torino, Einaudi, 1973.

— *Saggi critici*, traduzione di Lidia Lonzi, Torino, Einaudi, 1976.

Beach, Joseph Warren, *English Literature of the Nineteenth and the Early Twentieth Centuries – 1798 to the First World War*, New York, Collier Books, 1962.

Bell, Michael, "Introduction: Modern movements in literature", in *The Context of English Literature 1900–1930*, ed. Michael Bell, London, Methuen, 1980.

— ed., *The Context of English Literature 1900–1930*, London, Methuen, 1980.

Bennett, Arnold, *Accident*, Kelly Bray (UK), House of Stratus, 2008.

— *Anna of the Five Towns*, introduction by Frank Swinnerton, London, Penguin, 2001.

— "Books and Persons", *New Age*, VI (24 March 1910).

— *Books and Persons 1926–1931*, ed. Andrew Mylett, London and Hamden, CT, Archon Books, 1974.

— *Fame and Fiction. An Enquiry into Certain Popularities*, London, Grant Richards, 1901.

— *The Author's Craft*, London, New York, George H. Doran, 1914.

— *The Grim Smile of the Five Towns,* Harmondsworth, Penguin, 1946.

— *The Journals*, Harmondsworth, Penguin, 1971.

— *The Old Wives' Tale*, Oxford, Oxford University Press, 1995.

— *The Truth About an Author,* New York, George H. Doran, 1911.

Benjamin, Walter, *Angelus Novus: Saggi e frammenti*, traduzione di Renato Solmi, Torino, Einaudi, 1962.

Bergonzi, Bernard, "The Advent of Modernism" in *The Twentieth Century*, ed. Bernard Bergonzi, *Sphere History in the English Language*, 12 Vols., London, Sphere Books, 1970.

Besant, Walter, *The Art of Fiction*, New York, Cupples, Upham and Company, 1885.

Bloom, Harold, *The Western Canon*, New York, Riverhead Books, 1995.

Boulton, Marjorie, *The Anatomy of the Novel*, London and Boston, Routledge and Kegan Paul, 1975.

Bradbury, Malcolm and James McFarlane, "The Name and Nature of Modernism", in *Modernism: A Guide to European Literature 1890–1930*, ed. Malcolm Bradbury and James McFarlane, London and New York, Penguin, 1991.

Brugmans, Linette F., (Introduction et Notes par), *Correspondance André Gide-Arnold Bennett: Vingt ans d'Amitié Litteraire (1911–1931)*, Genève, Librairie Droz, 1964.

Bunyan, John, *The Pilgrim's Progress*. An Authoritative Text, ed. Cynthia Wall, New York and London, W. W. Norton, 2009.

Carey, John, *The Intellectuals and The Masses. Pride and Prejudice among the Literary Intelligentsia 1880–1939*, London and Boston, Faber and Faber, 1992.

Carter, Ian, *Railways and Culture in Britain: The Epitome of Modernity*, Manchester and New York, Manchester University Press, 2001.

Cheetham, J. Keith, *On the Trail of John Wesley*, Edinburgh, Luath Press, 2003.

Cosgrove, Denis, *Social Formation and Symbolic Landscape*, London, Crooms Helm, 1984.

Coustillas, Pierre, *The Heroic Life of George Gissing*, 3 vols., London, Pickering & Chatto, 2011–2011.

Cox, Sidney Hayes, "Romance in Arnold Bennett", *The Sewanee Review*, 28, 3 (July 1920).

David, Deirdre, *Intellectual Women and Victorian Patriarchy*, Ithaca, NY, Cornell University Press, 1987.

de Giovanni, Flora, "Virginia Woolf e le arti" in *Immagini/Pictures* di Virginia Woolf, traduzione, cura e introduzione di Flora de Giovanni, Napoli, Liguori Editore, 2002.

Dennis, Barbara, and David Skilton (eds.), *Reform and Intellectual Debate in Victorian England*, London and New York, Croom Helm, 1987.

Donovan, Patrick, *Arnold Bennett: Lost Icon*, Lewes, Unicorn, 2022.

Drabble, Margaret, *Arnold Bennett: A Biography*, London, Weidenfeld and Nicolson, 1974.

Eagleton, Terry, *Marxism and Literary Criticism*, London, Methuen, 1976.

— *Criticism and Ideology*, London, Verso, 1980.

— *Literary Theory: An Introduction*, Oxford, Basil Blackwell, 1983.

Ebbatson, Roger, *The Evolutionary Self. Hardy, Forster, Lawrence*, Brighton, The Harvester Press, 1982.

— *Landscape and Literature 1830–1914; Nature, Text, Aura*, London, Palgrave Macmillan, 2013.

Edel, Leon and Gordon N. Ray, ed., *Henry James and W. H. Wells: A Record of Their Friendship, Their Debate on the Art of Fiction, and Their Quarrel*, Urbana, IL, and London, University of Illinois Press, 1958.

Eliot, George, *Middlemarch*, ed. David Carroll, Oxford and New York, Oxford University Press, 1989.

Fletcher, John and Malcolm Bradbury, "The Introverted Novel", in *Modernism: A Guide to European Literature 1890–1930*, ed. Malcolm Bradbury and James McFarlane, London and New York, Penguin, 1991.

Ford, Boris, ed., *The New Pelican Guide to English Literature*, 8 vols., Harmondsworth, Penguin, 1986.

Forster, E. M., *Aspects of the Novel*, Harmondsworth, Penguin, 1972.

Fraser, G. S., *The Modern Writer and His World*, Harmondsworth, Penuin, 1972.

Frigerio, Francesca, *Modernismo e modernità: Per un ritratto della letteratura inglese 1900–1940*, Torno, Einaudi, 2014.

Furst, Lilian R. and Peter N. Skrine, *Naturalism*, London, Methuen, 1971.

Garnett, Edward, Review, *The Nation*, 21 November 1908.

Gill, Stephen, *Wordsworth and the Victorians*, Oxford and New York, Oxford University Press / Clarendon Press, 2001.

Hardy, Thomas, *Jude the Obscure*, Oxford, Oxford University Press, 2008.

Harvey, Geoffrey M., "Narrowing the Abyss: Arnold Bennett's *Anna of the Five Towns*", *Études Anglaises*, 60, 1 (2007).

Haddakin, Lilian, "Silas Marner", in *Critical Essays on George Eliot*, ed. Barbara Hardy, London, Routledge and Kegan Paul, 1970.

Headrick, Daniel R., *The Tools of Empire: Technology and European Imperialism in the Nineteenth Century*, New York, Oxford University Press, 1981.

Hepburn, James G., "Arnold Bennett, Romantic Realist", *Modern Philology*, 71, 2 (November 1973).

— *The Art of Arnold Bennett*, Bloomington, IN, Indiana University Press, 1963.

— (ed.), *The Letters of Arnold Bennett*, 4 voll., London, Oxford University Press, 1966–86.

Holloway, John, "The Literary Scene", *The New Pelican Guide to English Literature*, ed. Boris Ford, 8 vols., Harmondsworth, Penguin, 1986, *VII: From James to Eliot.*

Hoskins, W. G., *The Making of the English Landscape*, Harmondsworth, Penguin, 1983.

Hough, Graham, *Image and Experience: Studies in a Literary Revolution*, London, Duckworth, 1960.

Houghton, Walter E., *The Victorian Frame of Mind*, New Haven and London, Yale University Press, 1957.

Hynes, Samuel, "The Whole Contention between Mr. Bennett and Mrs. Woolf", *Novel*, 1, 1 (Autumn 1967).

Iser, Wolfgang, *The Act of Reading. A Theory of Aesthetic Response*, Baltimore and London, Johns Hopkins University Press, 1991.

James, Henry, *The Art of the Novel*, with an Introduction by R. P. Blackmur, New York, Charles Scribner's Sons, 1937.

Jordan, Jane and Andrew King, eds., *Ouida and Victorian Popular Culture*, Farnham and Burlington, VT, Ashgate, 2013.

Joyce, James, *Ulysses*, ed. Hans Walter Gabler with Wolfhard Steppe and Claus Melchior, Harmondsworth, Penguin, 1986.

Judson, A. C., "Arnold Bennett and the Five Towns", *Texas Review*, 8, 2 (January 1923).

Keating, Peter, *The Haunted Study. A Social History of the English Novel 1875–1914*, London, FontanaPress, 1991.

— *The Working Classes in Victorian Fiction*, London, Routledge and Kegan Paul, 1971.

Kettle, Arnold, *An Introduction to the English Novel*, 2 vols., London, Hutchinson, 1972.

Kermode, Frank, *Lawrence*, London, Fontana/Collins, 1973.

Kundera, Milan, *L'arte del romanzo*, Milano, Adelphi, 2003.

Laurence, Patricia Ondek, *The Reading of Silence: Virginia Woolf in the English Tradition*, Stanford, CA, Stanford University Press, 1991.

Leavis, F. R., *The Great Tradition: George Eliot, Henry James, Joseph Conrad*, Harmondsworth and New York, Penguin, 1983 [1a. ed. 1948].

Lodge, David, *Consciousness and the Novel*, London, Penguin, 2002.

— *The Modes of Modern Writing*, London, Edward Arnold, 1977.

— *Write On: Occasional Essays '65–'85*, London, Secker and Warburg, 1986.

Lubbock, Percy, *The Craft of Fiction*, New York, Viking, 1972 [1st ed. 1957].

Lucas, John, *Arnold Bennett. A Study of His Fiction*, London, Methuen, 1974.

Lukács, György, *The Historical Novel*, transl. by Hannah and Staley Mitchell, London, Merlin Press, 1989.

Marroni, Francesco, "Against the Victorian Grain: *Moths* as Verbal Excess and Epistemic Decapitation", *The Atlantic Critical Review*, 5, 2 (July-September 2009), pp. 18–34.

— "'A Great Grey Void': Henry James, le 'Prefaces' e i sentieri della critica", *Letterature d'America*, 19–20, 83–84 (1999–2000), pp. 31–58.

— *La verità difficile: uno studio sui romanzi di George Eliot*, Bologna, Pàtron, 1980.

— "Middlemarch e le metafore dell'eccesso", in *Middlemarch: il romanzo*, a cura di Anita Weston e John McRae, Napoli, Loffredo, 1987.

— "The Paradigm of Negativity in *Anna of the Five Towns*", *Cahiers Victoriens et Edouardiens*, 41 (avril 1995), pp. 99–120.

— "Thomas Hardy e la 'fine' del romanzo vittoriano", *Rivista di Studi Vittoriani*, 8, 16 (Luglio 2003), pp. 11–23.

— "Thomas Hardy e il silenzio della vecchiaia", in Sergio Ruffini e Clara Mucci (a cura di), *"O sir, you are old...": Riflessioni sulla vecchiaia a partire da Shakespeare*, Napoli, Edizioni Scientifiche Italiane, 1999, pp. 77–96.

Matthiessen, F. O., *American Renaissance: Art and Expression in the Age of Emerson and Whitman*, London/ Oxford/New York, Oxford University Press, 1974.

McFarlane, James, "The Mind of Modernism", in *Modernism: A Guide to European Literature 1890–1930*, ed. Malcolm Bradbury and James McFarlane, London and New York, Penguin, 1991.

Melchiori, Barbara e Giorgio, *Il gusto di Henry James*, Torino, Einaudi, 1974.

Miller, J. Hillis, *On Literature: Thinking in Action*, London and New York, Routledge, 2002.

Nussbaum, Martha C., *Poetic Justice: The Literary Imagination and Public Life*, Boston, Beacon Press, 2004.

O'Faolain, Sean, *The Short Story*, Cork and Dublin, The Mercier Press, 1989.

Ormerod, David, "Doorway and Windowframe: Aetheticism and the Iconography of Bennett's *Anna of the Five Towns*", *English Studies*, 2 (1997).

Ouida (Marie Louise de la Ramée), *Moths*, New York, Broadview Press, 2005.

— *Under Two Flags: A Story of the Household and the Desert*, Oxford, Oxford University Press, 1995.

Overton, J. H., *John Wesley*, London, Methuen, 1891.

Parrinder, Patrick, *Nation and the Novel: The English Novel from the Origins to the Present Day*, Oxford and New York, Oxford University Press, 2006.

Pollock, John, *Wesley The Preacher*, Eastbourne, Kingsway Publications, 2003.

Pontrandolfo, Luisa, *Railway Mania: Gioie e paure 'ferroviarie' nella letteratura inglese dell'Ottocento*, Bari, Edizioni B. A. Graphis, 2001.

Popp, Andrew, "'Though it is but a Promise': Business Probity in Arnold Bennett's *Anna of the Five Towns*", *Business History*, 48, 3 (July 2006).

Prince, Gerald, *Narratologia. La forma e il funzionamento della narrativa*, trad. di Mario Salvadori, Parma, Pratiche Editrice, 1984.

Riffaterre, Michael, *Semiotics of Poetry,* Bloomington, IN, Bloomington University Press, 1984.

Roberts, Andrew, "Culture and Consciousness in the Twentieth-century novel" in *Bloomsbury Guide to English Literature: The Twentieth Century*, ed. Linda R. Williams, London, Bloomsbury, 1994.

Said, Edward W., *Beginnings: Intentions and Method*, New York, Columbia University Press, 1985.

–– *The World, the Text and the Critic*, London, Vintage, 1991.

Saunders, Angharad, "Interpretation of an Interior", *Literary Geography*, 1, 2 (2015).

Segre, Cesare, *Intrecci di voci. La polifonia nella letteratura del Novecento*, Torino, Einaudi, 1991.

Siegel, Paul N., "Revolution and Evolution in Bennett's *The Old Wives Tale*", *Clio*, 4, 2 (1975).

Sisman, Adam, *The Friendship Wordsworth and Coleridge*, New York and London, Penguin, 2006.

Spilka, Mark, "Henry James and Walter Besant: 'The Art of Fiction' Controversy", *Novel*, 6, 2 (Winter 1973).

Squillace, Robert, *Modernism, Modernity, and Arnold Bennett*, Lewisburg, Bucknell University Press; London, Associated University Press, 1997.

Stade, George, ed., *Six Modern British Novelists*, New York, Columbia University Press, 1974.

Tawney, R. H., *Religion and the Rise of Capitalism. A Historical Study*, with a prefatory note by Dr Charles Gore, Harmondsworth, Penguin, [1922, 1926], 1972.

Tindall William York, *Forces in Modern British Literature 1885–1956*, New York, Vintage Books/Random House, 1956.

Tobin, Patricia Drechsel, *Time and the Novel: The Genealogical Imperative*, Princeton, NJ, Princeton University Press, 1978.

Tomkins, Stephen, *John Wesley: A Biography*, London, Lion Publishing, 2003.

Traversetti, Bruno e Stefano Andreani, *Incipit. Le tecniche dell'esordio nel romanzo europeo*, Torino, Nuova ERI, 1988.

Trollope, Anthony, *An Autobiography*, ed. Michael Sadleir and Frederick Page, Oxford, Oxford University Press, 1989.

Wain, John, *Arnold Bennett*, New York, Columbia University Press, 1967.

— "Arnold Bennett," in *Six Modern British Novelists*, ed. George Stade, New York, Columbia University Press, 1974.

— "Introduction", in Arnold Bennett, *The Old Wives's Tale*, London, Penguin, 2007.

— "Remarks on the Short Story", *Journal of the Short Story in English*, 41 (Autumn 2003).

Weber, Max, *L'etica protestante e lo spirito del capitalismo*, Firenze, Sansoni, 1977.

Wellek, René and Austin Warren, *Theory of Literature*, New York, Harcourt, Brace and Company, 1949.

Wells, H. G., *Experiment in Autobiography*, New York, Macmillan, 1934.

Weston, Anita e John McRae (a cura di), *Middlemarch: il romanzo*, Napoli, Loffredo, 1987.

Williams, Linda R. "Introduction: Writing from Modernism to Postmodernism", in *Bloomsbury Guide to English Literature: The Twentieth Century*, ed. Linda R. Willims, London, Bloomsbury, 1994.

Williams, Raymond, *Culture and Society 1780–1950*, Harmondsworth, Penguin, 1971.

— *The Country and the City*, London, Chatto and Windus, 1973.

Wilson, Harris, ed., *Arnold Bennett and H.G.Wells. A Record of a Personal and a Literary Friendship*, London, Rupert Hart-Davis, 1960.

Woolf, Virginia, "Mr. Bennett and Mrs. Brown", in *Collected Essays*, ed. Leonard Woolf, Vol. 1, London, Chatto & Windus, 1966, pp. 319–337.

Wordsworth, William, "Lines Composed a Few Miles above Tintern Abbey", *The Poems*, ed. John O. Hayden, 2 Voll., Harmondsworth, Penguin, 1977.
— *The Prelude. A Parallel Text*, ed J. C. Maxwell, Harmondsworth, Penguin, 1971.
Wright, Walter F., *Arnold Bennett: Romantic Realist*, Lincoln, University of Nebraska Press, 1971.
Young, Kenneth, *Arnold Bennett*, Harlow, Longman (for the British Council), 1975.
Zola, Émile, *Le roman expérimental*, Paris, Garnier-Flammarion, 1971.
Zulli, Tania, "L'alienazione dell'artista in 'The Death of Simon Fuge'", *Merope*, X, 24 (Maggio 1998), pp. 17–28.

Sitography

A History of the County of Stafford: Volume 8, ed. J G Jenkins (London, 1963), pp. 276–307. *British History Online*: http://www.british-hist ory.ac.uk/vch/staffs/vol8/pp276-307
Margaret Drabble, "A writer with Class" – *Times Literary Supplement* (13 May 2022): https://www.the-tls.co.uk/articles/arnold-bennett-lost-icon-patrick-donovan-book-review-margaret-drabble/
Simon Heffer, "Sadly, the snobs were right about Trollope", *The Telegraph,* 1 January 2011: http://www.telegraph.co.uk/comment/col umnists/simonheffer/8234543/Sadly-the-snobs-were-right-about-Trollope.html
Elizabeth Jones, "Work and Industry in *Anna of the Five Towns*", *Innervate*, vol. 2 (2009–2010), p. 259: https://www.nottingham.ac.uk/english/documents/innervate/09-10/0910joneseworkindustry.pdf
John Pridmore, *Church Times* (15 July 2022): https://www.churchti mes.co.uk/articles/2022/15-july/books-arts/book-reviews/arnold-bennett-lost-icon-by-patrick-donovan
http://shop.manchestergalleries.org/scapegoat-holman-hunt-giclee-print-119-p.asp

Taylor, D. J., Literary Review, Aug 2022. https://literaryreview.co.uk/
    from-staffordshire-to-the-savoy
John Wain, "Remarks on the Short Story", *Journal of the Short Story
    in English*, 41 (Autumn 2003): http://jsse.revues.org/index318.html
    http://www.thepotteries.org
http://www.methodistheritage.org.uk/heritageofmethodism.htm

INDEX OF NAMES

Victorian & Edwardian Studies

Edited by Francesco Marroni

The series focuses primarily on subjects, works and authors of Victorian and Edwardian literature in light of an interpretation of the lines of epistemic continuities/discontinuities involved in the historical notion of "the long nineteenth-century" (1789–1914). While promoting new critical perspectives in the field of Victorian textual production (from literature to visual arts, from scientific works to popular press), the series also aims to publish interdisciplin-ary works which consider the ideological and sociocultural implications of the radical transformation in Victorian society. The publications in the series originate mainly from research work conducted at the CUSVE (Centre for Victorian and Edwardian Studies – University of Pescara, Italy) but the series is open to contributions originating outside the CUSVE. It publishes monographs, collections of essays, conference proceedings and doctorial dissertations. The language of publications is both English and Italian.

Vol. 1   Francesco Marroni, Renzo D'Agnillo & Massimo Verzella (eds)
         Elizabeth Gaskell and the Art of the Short Story
         ISBN 978-3-0343-0678-2, 2011

Vol. 2   Tania Zulli
         *Colonial Transitions. Literature and Culture in the Late
         Victorian Age*
         ISBN 978-3-0343-1121-2, 2011

Vol. 3   Silvia Antosa
         Richard Francis Burton. Victorian Explorer and Translator
         ISBN 978-3-0343-1360-5, 2012

Vol. 4   Catherine Marshall & Stéphane Guy (eds)
         The Victorian Legacy in Political Thought
         ISBN 978-3-0343-1495-4, 2014

Vol. 5   Mariaconcetta Costantini
         Sensation and Professionalism in the Victorian Novel
         ISBN 978-3-0343-1588-3, 2015

Vol. 6   Renzo D'Agnillo
         Arthur Hugh Clough: The Poetry of a Questioning Spirit
         ISBN 978-3-0343-2418-2, 2017

Vol. 7   Elisa Bizzotto
         Mario Praz: Voice Centre Stage
         ISBN 978-3-0343-3344, 2019

Vol. 8   Francesca D'Alfonso
         Arnold Bennett's Fiction. From the Potteries to Literary Success
         ISBN 978-3-0343-4596-5, 2023